CARPE
SEIZE THE DAY
DIEM

TONY CAMPOLO

CARPE

SEIZE THE DAY

DIEM

WORD PUBLISHING
Dallas·London·Vancouver·Melbourne

CARPE DIEM

Unless otherwise indicated, Scripture quotations are from the King
James Version of the Bible.

The author expresses thanks for the use of this song and poem: "Class
of '57" by Don Reid and Harold Reid, copyright © 1972 House of
Cash Music (administered by Copyright Management, Inc.). All
rights reserved. International copyright secured. Used by permission.

"Listen to the Mustn'ts" from *Where the Sidewalk Ends* by Shel
Silverstein, © 1974 by Evil Eye Music, Inc. Reprinted by permission
of HarperCollins Publishers.

Library of Congress Cataloging-in-Publication Data

Campolo, Anthony.
Carpe diem/Tony Campolo
      p.   cm.
ISBN 0–8499-1008-0 (hardcover)
ISBN 0-8499-3680-2 (trade paper)
1. Christian life–1960–. I. Title.
BV4501.2.C24798 1994
248.4–dc20   93–48818
                                               CIP

Printed in the United States of America.

5 6 7 8 9 BVG 9 8 7 6 5 4 3 2 1

To Edwin F. Bailey,

a Kierkegaardian knight of faith
who showed a boy
the genius of being fully alive.

Contents

Preface

It was time for me to write this book. I'm fifty-eight years old, and I'm wondering where my life has gone. It seems to me that just as soon as my pimples cleared up, my hair fell out. All at once I feel like my life is on the final run, and I want to be sure that I get all that life has to offer out of what's left. That is why I decided to stop and reflect on what life is all about and what makes it worth living.

The question I want to answer in this book is whether or not my relationship with Jesus can help me in this quest. Can it really empower me to live my life "more abundantly"? Can it actually help me to experience life with a passion and joy?

In more everyday terms, I want life to be fun, and I want to know if Jesus can help make that happen. To some, that might sound a bit selfish and unreligious. Happiness, say the heavy theologians, is a superficial emotion. Maybe they are right. But that *is* what I want right now. I want to laugh a lot and to make other people laugh. I want to enjoy my kids and to play with my grandchildren. And most of all I want the time that I spend with my wife to be rich and gratifying.

I've always preached about Jesus and what He can do for those who embrace the life that He offers. I have talked about how giving yourself away in love to the poor and the oppressed yields a spiritual ecstasy that will leave you grateful for the privilege. I have declared how living in intimate fellowship with the resurrected Christ creates an aliveness and an awareness that makes people talk of experiencing eternal life right here and now. But there are times when I stop and ask myself if all of this is true. That is how I came to write this book. And in the pages that follow, I want to share my answers with you.

To do all of this, I needed a lot of help. I am grateful to Karen King, my secretary, who punched my written words into a word processor. Pat Carroll and Linda Wychers are two special people who work with Karen in the office. They help make it possible for her to squeeze typing this book into all the other work I give her to do.

But most of all there is my best friend for the last thirty-five years—my wife, Peggy. She not only does a lot of encouraging, she also has been the first editor on most of what I write. By the time she finishes with a manuscript, I almost come across as literate!

I'm nervous about this book, so write and let me know how you like it—that is, if you do like it. If you don't like it, it's still OK to write, even if I won't be as thrilled to get your letter. Either way, thanks for reading it.

Tony Campolo
Eastern College
St. David's, Pennsylvania 19087

PART I

THE BOOK,
THE AUTHOR,
AND THE PROBLEM
OF DEADNESS

1

The Book

*H*ow long have you lived?"

I posed the question to the students on the first day of a special seminar course on existentialism.

No one answered. It may have been that my manner was intimidating. But then again, maybe it was because the question had a certain ambiguity to it.

So I picked out one of the students on the front row of the lecture hall and, riveting my attention on him, I asked the question again, this time with an intensely personal emphasis.

"How long have *you* lived?" I asked.

My inquiry must have seemed like an attack on him. I could see that he was taken aback. The question seemed to pull him out of a time of private reverie. Instinctively he answered, "Twenty-four years!"

"No! No!" I responded. "I didn't ask you how long you have existed as a breathing, functioning member of the human race. I wanted you to tell me how long you have been really alive."

I could tell that this poor, besieged student was befuddled. I sensed he had some inkling of what I was getting at. But he wasn't sure. I knew he needed some help.

"When I was twelve years old," I told him, "I was taken to New York. It was one of those cultural enrichment trips that was designed to broaden the experiences of the sixth-grade class. There must have been close to forty of us in the group, although I don't remember enough about it to say for sure. What I do remember was being on the observation deck near the top of the Empire State Building. I had been running around chasing somebody just for the fun of it, as kids on a school trip are prone to do, when I stopped, went over to the guardrail, took hold of it, and gazed over the city.

"I remember that moment vividly. Everything around me seemed to drop away. A strange stillness drowned out the noise of the other kids. For me that moment belonged to another dimension of time and space. And I took it in—that incredible city, sprawled out before me with its towers of concrete and glass. There was an awesome expanse of what seemed to be a vast, miniaturized, make-believe, toy world. It was like looking at one of those model railroad displays you see in department stores at Christmas, only infinitely larger.

"I was awestruck! Full of wonder! And I remember saying these simple words to myself: *Tony! You are on top of the Empire State Building.*

"It was with a heightened awareness, a hyper-intensive consciousness, that I held that moment far too wonderful to describe. In a mystical way, I stepped outside of myself at that moment and reflected upon myself experiencing it.

"I do not know how long I will live," I told my student, "but if I were to live a million years, I would remember *that* moment, because I truly *lived* it."

"Now, let me ask you the question again," I said. "How long have you lived?"

The young man had been moved to serious reflection, and he responded very slowly, as though he were carefully weighing each word of his answer: "When you talk about living like you lived that particular moment in New York, maybe a minute. Maybe two! I mean, if I were to add up all those times when I experienced life with that kind of heightened awareness, they are not likely to come out to much more than that!"

Then he added a regretful afterthought. "When I stop to think about it, most of my life has been the meaningless passage of time between all too few moments when I have really been alive."

Even so, life for this young man was probably better than for most people. For, were the truth to be known, most people are born and years later die without really having lived at all. There are those who never reflect with any intensive awareness on any part of their lives. They eat and sleep, they work and reproduce, and they study and forget. They play it safe and tiptoe through life with no aspiration other than to arrive at death safely.

Life in the Face of Death

Every once in a while, something happens that shakes people out of such a mundane existence and introduces them to the ecstasy that lies waiting with hidden potential to be discovered in everyday life. It was such a something that changed the life of the nineteenth-century Russian novelist Fyodor Dostoyevsky. He had never been an ordinary man, but it was the experience of a particular moment that gave him the insight that was so much a part of his genius.

As a young idealist, Dostoyevsky believed that political revolution was the essential route for the life God willed for him. He joined one of the militant socialist movements that seemed to be omnipresent in nineteenth-century Russia. But his efforts to create the kingdom of God by overthrowing the czar came to naught, as his mini-revolution failed. He was imprisoned by the czar and, so he thought, sentenced to death.

But he didn't die!

Those who challenged the czar's totalitarian power were sometimes subjected to a cruel psychological trick designed to break their spirits. They were blindfolded and put before a firing squad. The commands of, "Ready! Aim! Fire!" were given. The sound of shots would ring out. But then—nothing! The bullets were blanks. The victims had been forced to go through the agony of dying, but then there was not the deliverance that death itself can bring.

The painful process was designed to destroy the emotional life of the czar's victims, but in the case of Dostoyevsky it ironically provided a whole new way of living it. Facing death without dying gave him a new perception of reality and an ability to apprehend life with an appreciative passion. As the moment which he was sure would be his last approached, he found himself living life with a hitherto-unknown heightened awareness. In the face of death, each event that remained in his existence, regardless of how apparently ordinary, took on momentous importance.

As he ate his last meal, he concentrated on the taste of every bite, savoring each morsel, because he believed this would be the last food he would ever eat.

As they marched him into the courtyard where he was to be executed, he took in the sun and breathed the air with an intensive appreciation he had never known before.

To the condemned Dostoyevsky, every sensation was enjoyed with a heightened awareness. Each experience was felt with a powerful sensitivity.

He studied the face of each and every soldier charged with the grisly task of shooting him, because these, he was convinced, were the last faces he would ever see.

Dostoyevsky was *living* in the face of death. Later, he would confess that he had lived more in what he had been convinced were the last moments of his life than he had ever lived before. Each moment and each experience leading up to that mock execution had been seized with a passion, and he had tried to suck out of what remained of life all that it possibly could give. He had learned in the face of death to live out the ancient Latin admonition *Carpe Diem!* (Seize the day!)

The Strange Childhood of R. Buckminster Fuller

One other story immediately comes to mind as I try to define this special kind of passion for life I believe to be at the core of ultimate spirituality. It is a story that comes from the life of a man whom many consider to be one of the truly creative minds of the twentieth century, R. Buckminster Fuller. This man, whose inventiveness seems to have known no bounds, was the one who dreamed up the geodesic dome, along with a whole host of other innovations. So numerous are his achievements that a list of his inventions would fill a good-sized book.

Fuller explained that the source of his creativity was a painful misfortune that had occurred during his childhood. He described how, as a small child, he lost his sight. He went to bed one night able to see and awoke the next morning blind. Medical experts were not able to explain the cause of his horrific and sudden blindness. There was no reason for it. It just happened.

For several years the child remained blind. Then, just as suddenly and as inexplicably as he had lost his sight, he regained it. Without any indication as to what was coming, one morning he woke up able to see again.

In retrospect, Fuller explained, that tragic time proved to be a blessing in disguise. When he regained his sight, he claims that he saw everything entirely differently than he would have if his temporary blindness had not happened. He contended that society had trained him to view the world in a taken-for-granted fashion. But the hold society had on him had been broken by his blindness.

Upon regaining his sight, the world proved miraculously new and strangely wonderful to him. Along with his renewed vision, he put to use the creative imagination developed during his years of blindness. Fuller's visual re-engagement with the world was accomplished by a sense of awe and a new passion for discovery that others seldom know. He claimed his excitement for life was intensified beyond anything that would have been possible had he always been able to see.

This book is about the special kind of aliveness and awareness that Fyodor Dostoyevsky and R. Buckminster Fuller knew. It is about engaging the world as I momentarily experienced it as a twelve-year-old boy atop the Empire State Building. It is an attempted exploration into the kind of heightened experience that goes beyond happiness and is hinted at in the biblical promise of joy.

This book is about being "in Christ" in a spiritual and emotional way. It is about a special kind of ecstasy that can be experienced when by God's grace we come to see things our natural eyes alone could never see. It is about a new dimension to life where we hear those things previously drowned out by the mundane sounds of this world.

Most of all, this is a book about Jesus. It is about this man sent by God who promises a born-again experience to anyone who surrenders to a mystical invasion by His Spirit.

It is about this Jesus who once said to us:

"I am come that they might have life, and that they might have it more abundantly." (John 10:10b)

It is about this Jesus who came to dispel the deadness. He is the One who even now offers to be an energizing presence within us, a presence that can enable us to dance in the midst of a tired-out world. And it is about this Jesus who is the light that can overcome the darkness of our lives.

Consider these incredible claims that He makes for Himself:

"I am the resurrection, and the life." (John 11:25)
"I am the light of the world." (John 9:5)
"I am the door." (John 10:9)
"I am that bread of life." (John 6:48)

Don't ignore Jesus' wildly hopeful promises. For anyone whose soul is dry, there is the good news He once gave to a woman He met by a well:

"Whosoever drinketh of the water that I shall give him shall never thirst: but the water that I shall give him shall be in him a well of water springing up into everlasting life." (John 4:14)

For that person who seems too encumbered to enjoy life, there is His relieving invitation:

"Come unto me, all ye that labour and are heavy laden, and I will give you rest." (Matt. 11:28)

And for anyone who feels confused about where to turn to find fire for a heart that has lost all its warmth, He boldly declares:

"I am the way, the truth, and the life." (John 14:6)

Those who have given themselves over to this Savior give ample testimonies as to what He can do. His one-time enemy, Paul of Tarsus, had no reservations when he wrote:

I know whom I have believed, and am persuaded that he is able to keep that which I have committed unto him against that day. (2 Tim. 1:12b)

And Paul assures us:

If any man be in Christ, he is a new creature: old things are passed away; behold, all things are become new. (2 Cor. 5:17)

His apostle John also bore witness to what His power could do:

In him was life; and the life was the light of men. And the light shineth in darkness; and the darkness comprehended it not. (John 1:4–5)

The testimonies about the miraculous new life He will give to those who are ready to be open to the infilling of His Spirit are so numerous that John once wrote:

And there are also many other things which Jesus did, the which, if they should be written every one, I suppose that even the world itself could not contain the books that should be written. (John 21:25)

This book is about the new life in Christ!

2

The Author

I have been accused of being a speaker who appeals to people's emotions. And to that charge I gladly plead guilty.

Emotion is what life is all about for me. As far as I'm concerned, those rationalists with their computer-like minds seem to have lost most of their humanity. And those pseudointellectual sophomores at the university who scoff at my passion don't get it when I say, "I feel; therefore, I am."

Call it my Italian temperament if you will, but to me to live is to laugh and dance. It is to embrace the tragic with desperate tears and to give myself to love with intensive abandon. To me, living is to know both the agony and ecstasy of human existence and to disdain that emotional no man's land where moderate citizens know neither the heights nor the depths of the human condition.

I've always been this way. Back in my college days I remember a time when I was leaving the theater after seeing Anthony Quinn in *Zorba the Greek* when my date told me she did not like the movie.

Furthermore, she said she did not like people like Anthony Quinn. As far as she was concerned, Zorba's emotionalism made him a very distasteful character.

I told my date right then and there we had come to the end of our relationship. If she wasn't into passion, I explained to her, she would never understand me. And if she didn't like Zorba, I said, then I could never relate to her with any depth.

A Philosophy of Life

It is not just my Italian temperament that makes me this way (although I will not deny that genes play a part in it). Actually, it is much more complicated than that. It has to do with a philosophy of life. It has to do with what I believe is essential to being human.

I believe that passion provides the way for us to express the most profound dimensions of human existence. I believe that our identities are established to the degree that we become passionately committed persons. I also believe that passion is the ultimate and only effective means to enter into a relationship with God or to know anything about God.

On this latter point I usually run into conflicts with my religious colleagues. Most of them believe it is through the intellect, rather than through the passionate heart, that spiritual depth is gained. My sometimes friends and would-be members of the intelligentsia look upon my passion with a certain amount of disdain. For them God is best discussed in sophisticated terms like "the Unmoved Mover" of Aristotle, "the Ground of all Being" of Paul Tillich, and "the Transcendental Categorical Imperative" as described by Immanuel Kent.

I am convinced that my intellectual friends make a very crucial mistake because they are more into the Greek philosophical tradition than they are into the biblical faith. And it is because they are heirs of the Greek philosophers instead of the Hebrew prophets that they view God in such a static and rational fashion. The Jews, you see, never considered Yahweh to be like that. For the people of Israel, God was a person who loved like a Father loves His children. To them He was a God of intense emotions. He was a God who could hate and be angry.

He was a God who could weep and laugh. He was a God who could change His mind when moved by pity and feel self-satisfaction when pleased with His creation.

What is even more important is to recognize that that same God is the God who desires passion from His people. He wants us to know Him through love rather than through reason, and He laughs at our arrogant attempts to try to grasp Him in intellectual terms. The simplest shepherd whose heart burned with passion for his God, such as the prophet from Takoa, was assumed by the Jews to know more about God than some educated scholar whose heart was not spent in emotional empathy with his Creator. The God of ancient Israel was a God who delighted in revealing Himself to the simple-minded who had "a pure and steadfast heart." It was in spontaneous worship marked by wild gyrating dancing that King David pleased his God. And it was in graphically exotic terms that the writer of the Song of Solomon blurred the line between communion with God and the ecstasy of sex.

My more rational friends never do seem able to figure out what the Song of Solomon is doing in the Bible. Religion for them has no relationship to the sensual passions of that biblical book. They just don't get it.

It is in this context that I readily accept my colleagues' accusation that my preaching and teaching are marked by emotionalism. I consider the charge to be a badge of honor.

Love and Reason

I do not want to convey the idea that in my relationship with God I have abandoned reason. To the contrary, I am thoroughly convinced that Christianity requires us to bring our brains along when we approach the throne of grace. "Having a reason for the faith that lies within us" is a directive coming from none other than the apostle Paul. I accept the role of reason in my faith. It is just that I believe intensely that the use of reason is to come in after passionate love has provided the first real taste of God. I concur with Blaise Pascal (hardly an intellectual lightweight), who while probing for God in the empirical and rational categories of science and logic came to know Him in the emotional transport of a mystical conversion. He wrote in his diary:

> On Monday, twenty-third of November . . . from about half-past ten in the evening until about half-past twelve

> Fire

> God of Abraham, God of Isaac, God of Jacob, not of the philosophers and scholars. Certitude! Certitude! Feeling! Joy! Peace! God of Jesus Christ.

In the final analysis, I believe we *feel* our way to God. Reason, I say, can take us only so far. It is out of the certainties of the heart, not the certainties of the mind, that we find the courage to make the leap of faith to ultimate truth. I believe it is through passionate love rather than well-reasoned syllogism that we come to know God. Rational descriptions and explanations are OK for people who are into religion, but they should come only after those people experience passionate love and faith.

In the end, theology is an attempt to put into sensible, objective terms a highly subjective encounter with God. It is an attempt to put into words what cannot be described, but is attempted nevertheless to encourage others to risk themselves in a similar leap of faith. But all who have passionately embraced God and who know the truth that comes in such a love affair readily admit, as Pascal wrote, "the heart has reasons which reason can never know." The knowledge of God that comes from passionate, loving surrender is a contrast to our puny thinking; it makes prideful scholarship a lot of foolishness (Rom. 1:21–22). We find God in the mystical revelations that come and go like the wind (John 3:8). The One who is the way, the truth, and the life (John 14:6) will not be reduced to our logical categories and intellectual formulas.

In our relationship with God reason is always only a helper to passionate love; it is never on the throne. We experience Him by totally abandoning ourselves to whatever He, through His Spirit, wants to do in us and through us. He refuses to be an object that we can observe and comprehend in detached, logical thought. God wants a passionate love for Himself, not a philosophically logical theology.

A Wild Love for God

There is a passionate love for God that He creates in us when we surrender to Him. It is this wild love for Him that is not only the basis for any real knowledge we have of God, but also the basis for a whole new way we can look at life. The God who calls us into an intensely personal and passionate relationship with Him transforms us through that relationship so that we encounter everything else in our lives conditioned by that passion.

This book is about those changes. It is about how those who allow themselves to be permeated with God's love experience all of life differently. It is about a whole new way of living.

Passion, for the converted, is expressed and experienced in everything that is done and in all of life's encounters. We feel it in the way we worship, in the way we make love, and in the way we play. The way we experience nature is marked by this passion. Everything, from the ways we taste food to the ways in which we read poetry, becomes intensely alive for the converted. All of life is lifted up so that in Christ we encounter it with a new awareness. This new and higher level of living is the abundant life Jesus promised (John 10:10b).

When I say that in Christ everything changes, I do not claim that everything we *do* will change. What I am saying is that everything we do will be done differently because it is felt differently. The same old things will no longer be the same old things. Objectively, everything may appear to remain the same, but subjectively, nothing will be the same. The convert is one who has learned how to seize life and experience it as God intended:

> If any man be in Christ, he is a new creature: old things are passed away; behold, all things are become new. (2 Cor. 5:17)

For the convert the same things are no longer the same things. In Christ everything is experienced in a new way . . . the way God wanted them to be experienced.

Irenaeus once said, "The glory of God is a man who is fully alive." This is what salvation is all about—and what this book is all about. It is not about a new life you can know in another world when this one is ended. It is about an aliveness you can experience in this life's ugly world with all its troubles and limitations.

But before I get you to explore the good news about all that goes with this new life in Christ, I want you to consider why it is that most people we meet in the here and now of everyday living seem devoid of not only this new life in Christ, but of any life at all. I want you to take a good look at this present age and what it is doing to people like you and me. I want you to give some thought to those who are caught up in the ways contemporary society prescribes for us. We need to take a look at what's going on in most people's lives and what it is doing to them. It is in contrast to the bad news about what is happening to these people that the good news about what is happening to those who are in Christ shines most brilliantly.

Before we consider the new life in Christ, let's take a good look at the inability to experience life and the tendency to deadness in this modern age.

3

The Problem We Must Face: A Sickness unto Death

*T*his age will die, not from sin, but from lack of passion." The quote comes from Soren Kierkegaard, a philosopher who was able to predict the maladies of our times more than a century ago. Everywhere I turn, I find validations for Kierkegaard's diagnosis. There is a deadness to our lives that seems everywhere evident.

Annually, marriages end by the millions. And they do not end for reasons we might imagine. Adultery is not even close to being the dominant cause for these failed love affairs, even though many married people have affairs. It is simply that the relationships die. And they die because the people are dead. After a handful of years, there isn't much passion left in these marriages. There isn't even enough passion for the betrayed spouses to hate their unfaithful mates. Hating takes emotion, and there just isn't much of that left in people these days. One-time partners calmly talk about "drifting apart." They describe themselves in the psychobabble so common on the "Donahue" show. They talk about having transcended "codependent relationships" and enjoying their "private space." Their marriages end amicably because there is so little caring left in either husbands or wives that there is nothing left to fight about—except money.

Pervasive Apathy

And the kids are dead. I used to like to be a speaker for high school assemblies, but I don't enjoy them anymore. It's not that the kids misbehave or show no respect. It's that they scare me with their deadness. In the old days, I could count on them to act up. I went to them expecting paper airplanes to come gliding down from the balcony and now and then a stink bomb to go off. But nowadays, the kids just sit there, dead. The blank looks on their faces never give away how they are feeling. Indeed they feel very little. This isn't a jaundiced outlook on life. Ask the kids themselves. They'll tell you. *Apathy* is the word they use. And any attempt to call a meeting to deal with the problem will probably have to be canceled due to lack of interest.

The kids have a word for it. They describe themselves as being "cool." I can hardly believe it. They talk about being "cool" as a virtue. And they are cool about everything. They have sex without real emotional involvement. They say cruel things to people without concern. Their mothers may cry at their unfeeling manners, and they hardly notice the tears. They can even kill without feeling.

I read a newspaper story about a teenager who lured a classmate into some high grass, raped and murdered her, then coolly went back to class. The story included a line that has become all too common in cases of this sort: "And when the verdict was read, the defendant showed no emotion." It would have been wholly erroneous if the newspaper had referred to the crime as an "act of passion." If there was anything it *wasn't*, it wasn't an act of passion. The kid was too cool for such a description.

I have to differ with the poet who claimed that most people live out their lives in "quiet desperation." I don't see it that way. *Desperation* is too strong a word. It has intensity to it, and I see little intensity. Instead I see men like trees, walking. I watch women at tea who "come and go / Talking of Michelangelo." Desperation is a feeling, and no feeling is there.

We also see apathy in politics.

The only concern these days seems to be with the economy. If there are enough dollars around to pay for the distractions that keep us from reflecting on the deadness of our souls, then nothing else concerns us. We watch the ethnic cleansing in Bosnia for a few minutes then we change channels, not because we are horrified—horror is profound emotion—but because we're bored.

Even our churches are dead. I have heard them criticized for not proclaiming the gospel, for not being relevant to the contemporary world, and for taking unpopular liberal positions on social issues. But the real reason mainline churches are emptying is because they are dead. Don't argue with me about this. Just go into most churches, and you'll *feel* the deadness.

You shouldn't blame it on the minister either. It starts with the people in the pews. I have watched them suck the life out of preachers with their deadness. Congregations take dreamers fresh out of seminary, deflate them, drain them of their energy, and hang them out to dry. No young pulpiteer can go on cajoling and pleading, raging and painting verbal pictures of a kingdom waiting to be born, without a sense that people care. Preachers today get little response. There is an absence of energy in the congregation, so the people can't respond. Even frantic preachers usually encounter only a sea of indifference. The expressionless faces give hardly a hint that anyone is registering the concerns of these would-be prophets.

Friedrich Nietzsche, the German existentialist philosopher, writes of a madman who charges into the marketplace of a medieval town, leaps onto the steps of the cathedral, then cries out to the crowd, "I want a requiem mass! I want a requiem mass! I want a requiem mass!"

"Who has died?" the people ask.

"God is dead!" the madman answers.

And when the crowd mocks his seemingly absurd announcement of the death of God, the madman retorts, "If God is not dead, then why have the churches become mortuaries?"

What Nietzsche should have realized is that it is not God who has died, but His people.

PART II

HOW WE GOT THIS WAY

4

Living at the End of History

*T*here's an essay that's hot right now in academic circles. It was writ-ten by Francis Fukuyama, a scholar in one of those Washington think-tanks. The name of the essay is "The End of History."

It is Fukuyama's thesis that human history is nothing more than a succession of nations, each of which gives life and expression to a great idea. He is what the philosophers call a neo-Hegelian. He believes that ideas are the driving force of history. Each of the great nations that have led human progress has taken hold of some great idea and organized those nations' lives and institutions around it. For a while each nation in turn would become what Fukuyama calls a "lead society," taking cen-ter stage and becoming the dominant force in molding society. But the role of leadership is only for a little while. Waiting to be born is a new nation that will give expression to some new idea with a new social structure and a new way of life built around it.

History unfolded in this way, according to Fukuyama, until America was born. America, he says, marks the end of history because in its institutions and value system the last great idea of the human experiment has been articulated. In America we have found the final expression of the spiritual force of history. Fukuyama tells us that Americans are the people who incarnate the latest and greatest belief system of human civilization.

We are the future! Social prophets argue that a hundred years from now democratic capitalism will be alive and well, and universally embraced. The future will be what America is in the present, only more so.

Consider the fact that most of the other countries of the world have taken to emulating America. The new nations formed out of the Soviet Union for the most part, aspire to our way of life. They are imitating our free-market economy as best they can, and they are trying to figure out how our kind of democracy can work for them. In the nations of Africa and Latin America, democratic capitalism may be hard to implement, but in the rhetoric of their leaders our socioeconomic system is still held up as the ideal.

This, of course, is heady stuff. It is the kind of stuff that, on the one hand, feeds the arrogance of the obnoxious "ugly American." But on the other hand it stirs us to reflection. The reality of history is that the two major ideological challenges to our philosophy of life have both faded from the scene. There was fascism during the thirties and, more recently, Marxist communism. Both of these challenges to democratic capitalism have been blown out of the water. They came, they saw, but they certainly did not conquer. When the dust cleared, the American ideology came out alive and well while these other "great ideas" seemed doomed to the trash heap of history.

Super nationalists will send up a cheer and declare, "We won! The cold war is over, and we are the victors." But before we all go into fits of rapture, we should ask *why* we won. What made our ideology the undisputed champion of the world?

I think we have to admit that it is not that our way of life is morally superior. Those who say that Marxist communism was nothing more than godless materialism have not taken serious stock of our

American way of life. If we did some serious reflecting few of us would argue that we have the most materialistic society in modern history. And the fact that most of us go to church and huge proportions of our citizenry claim to be "born again" does not alter that fact. Nor can we claim that we defeated our ideological enemies because we are smarter than they are. Intelligence has nothing to do with it. No, I think we are likely to agree that the real basis of our success is that the democratic system has proven itself to be the most effective means for creating an effective economy. Our factories have produced more things at a lower cost than any other system ever devised. In pragmatic terms, our system works despite all of its inequities and despite charges that America is imperialistic and environmentally irresponsible. Despite all the talk about our decadence, we still are the envy of the planet when it comes to economic success.

How We Created an Absurd World

The reason why the Commies did not beat us is simple. We out-produced them. Our socioeconomic system proved superior. The shelves of the shops in the Communist-bloc nations were bare while the shelves of our stores were packed with an array of consumer goods that defied description.

Dollar for dollar, we are able to buy more things and make more things for more of our people than any other society. Ours has been described by sociologists as *the* consumer society. And we've got the goods and the dispositions to buy them to prove it. America can outproduce, outsell, and outbuy anybody anytime and anywhere. And if the Japanese seem to be beating us at our own game these days, it is only because they have become *more* American than America. They have adopted our technology and organizational schemes, and even our baseball. Most important, they adopted our work ethic just as we became tired of it. In short, they are outdoing us at being us.

In order to keep our incredibly successful system working, there is something very important we Americans have to do. Buy! We have to buy the stuff that our system produces. And we have to keep on buying.

The megatons of consumer goods that flow out of our factories annually must be purchased fast and furiously. If they are not, factories will close, workers will become unemployed, and everything will stop. There is no doubt that the continued success of our way of life requires that we Americans become unrestrained consumers.

But there is a major problem in all of this. And that is that those of us who have the money to buy all the stuff that our factories produce already have everything we need. I didn't say, "Everything we want." I said, "Everything we need." There is no question about it. We have become a people whose needs are more than gratified; our essential hungers are more than satiated.

If people like you and me, whose needs have already been met, are going to keep America going, we are going to have to buy what we don't need. And we are going to have to buy what we don't need in larger and larger quantities. As absurd as all of this may seem, the survival of our way of life depends on this.

Just think about last Christmas season. Your biggest problem was probably not figuring out where you would get enough money to buy presents for family members and friends. Instead, it was trying to figure out what to buy for people who had *everything*. The answer to that problem should have been self-evident. What you should buy for those who have everything, is *nothing*. But you didn't have the guts to pull it off, did you?

No!

Instead you went up and down the aisles of department stores having anxiety attacks. Panic-stricken, you searched, yea, even prayed, that somebody somewhere had invented some new things that nobody needs so you could buy them for people who have everything. This is not an absurd description of a reasonable world. It is a rational description of an absurd world.

5

Buying into Needless Absurdity

*T*he absurdity of people buying things that nobody needs in order to give them to people who already have everything might be laughable except for its near-tragic consequences. The tragedy is that it takes a lot of money to buy all of these things nobody needs, and in order to get that money most of us neglect what is really important in being human. We do not have time for meaningful relationships. We have to work day and night if we are going to keep up with the demands for gratifying the artificially created wants that now haunt our psyche.

Husbands and wives do not have time to relate meaningfully anymore. Typically, the American married couple spends about eleven and a half minutes a day in any kind of conversation. This includes such "meaningful" exchanges as, "Pass the salt!" or "Did you bring in the paper?" We do not have time to relate because it takes most of our time working at jobs that most of us dislike just so we can have enough money to get all these things nobody wants. It is an interesting side

CARPE DIEM

note that most people really do not like what they feel they have to do in order to earn a living. According to one survey, more than 72 percent of us Americans wish we had different jobs.

The Real Cost of Buying What We Don't Need

I believe marriages fall apart primarily for this reason: in meeting the hectic, everyday demands of making a living, husbands and wives just do not have enough time to work out the tensions that are a normal part of marital relationships. They lack the time required for two people to get to know each other and, worse than that, they do not have the time to invest in creating love. As the years pass, people change, but they forget to tell each other because they are so busy earning enough money to buy the things they do not need. And so couples become strangers. Two people share the same bed but little else. She goes about life alone and so does he, and the marriage proves to be little more than two people who are alone together for a few minutes a day.

Kids also suffer from all of this. Even more sad than the reality that a typical American husband interacts with his wife for eleven and a half minutes a day is the discovery that he only talks to his children about four and a half minutes a day. Compare the amount of time that he talks to his children with the amount of time those children sit in front of a television set. According to conservative estimates, our kids watch television for five hours a day. If a child watches TV for five hours a day and talks to his father for four and a half minutes a day, it is easy to figure out which of the two has the greatest impact in forming the child's values and outlook on life. When some father tells me with an air of desperation, "I don't know where my kid comes up with some of his crazy ideas," I am prone to respond, "That's easy to figure out."

We don't have time to raise kids. While bringing up children should be a dual-parent responsibility, most sociologists agree that there is still some kind of special bond between mothers and their children. For reasons that may be based in part on hormones, the mother's love seems to have a unique role to play in the development of emotionally stable

— 38 —

boys and girls. Consequently, I have some problems accepting the practice of putting kids in day care.

Please don't get me wrong. I believe in day care. I have to. In a society in which almost half of the children are being raised in single-parent families, day care is an absolute necessity. It is day care that is making it possible for millions of single parents to earn enough to keep themselves and their children above the poverty line. But what is difficult for me to figure out is why people would *want* to put a child in day care when it isn't absolutely necessary. Don't they have an intense desire to hear the child's first words? Don't they want to see the eager little one take those first awkward steps?

Studies by social scientists make it difficult to argue with the claim that during the first few years of life, children are so imprinted by the adults who interact with them that the effects are difficult to undo. The way children think, their basic orientation toward life, their dispositions toward other people, and their capacity for trust and hope as well as an array of other traits are set in place during these formative years. Why would anyone turn over such an important stage of personality formation to relative strangers unless it were absolutely necessary?

The pressure on families to have both parents gainfully employed outside the home is great. In order to get the money to buy the stuff nobody needs, there is an overwhelming sense that married couples putting their kids in day care is a reasonable and necessary thing to do. After all, how else can both of them go to their jobs in industry and business? How else can they be free to earn enough money to get the things they *think* they need? These husbands and wives can be expected to tell us, "People can't get by on one salary alone anymore." They are right, of course, if by "getting by" they mean buying those things that are nothing more than the artificial wants that societal pressure has misled them into viewing as genuine needs.

Even in sophisticated circles where people ought to know better, those who have made staying home and raising children a priority are often made to feel that their lives are being wasted and that they could be doing "more significant things." When I was a member of the sociology faculty at an Ivy League university, my wife and I were expected to attend get-togethers with my colleagues and their spouses. On more than one occasion someone would ask my wife in what appeared to me to be a condescending manner, "And what is it you do, my dear?"

My wife, who is one of the most articulate persons I know, found a perfect response for such occasions. In machine gun fashion, she would reply, "I am socializing two *homo sapiens* into the dominant values of the Judeo-Christian tradition so they might be transformers of the social order into the kind of eschatological utopia God willed for us from before the foundation of the earth."

Then she would smile and ask, "And what is it *you* do?"

The inquirer would usually look flustered and, rather meekly say something like, "I teach sociology."

Raising children is the noblest of all vocations. This isn't rhetoric that should be sounded solely on Mother's Day. It's the truth! And it's about time we send that message loud and clear to a people who seem to have forgotten it.

I remember a married couple sitting in my office at Eastern College painfully confronting the reality that their nineteen-year-old daughter had not only lost her virginity and become pregnant, but had been so promiscuous she couldn't possibly figure out who the baby's father might be. With tears running down her cheeks, the distraught mother turned to her daughter and pitifully sobbed, "How could you do this to us . . . " (and the next words were completely predictable:) "after all we've done for you?"

That was not the time to ask that mother the simple question, "And just what is it you did for her?"

If I had asked, that mother probably would have gone through a long list of all the things she and her husband had worked so hard to be able to buy for their daughter. I probably would have heard about stereos, clothes, and even a car. And it all would have been said without the realization that in the exhaustive struggle to provide for their daughter what society had conditioned them to believe she had to have, they had failed to provide their daughter with what she really needed: available, loving parents. Parents who had time to be there for her, to listen to her, and to sense the growing turmoil in a teenager's life. These two people had had little time and energy to give their mixed-up daughter what she needed most of all: themselves. I wondered how much of the sexual promiscuity of that sad collegian had been an attempt by a lonely child to get her parents to pay attention to her.

6

What Fuels the Machine: Advertising

All of this leads us to one intriguing question: How do they get us to do it? How is it possible that fairly intelligent people should buy into such an absurd system? By what means do they get folks like us to exhaust ourselves, neglect our love life, ignore our children, and become the most stressed-out people in human history—all in an effort to get what we don't really need? What drives us to work so hard in order to buy things for people who already have everything?

The answer may seem overly simplistic, but it is, nevertheless, true. The answer is advertising. It is advertising that has made the gratification of artificially created wants more important than the satisfaction of our real needs. It is advertising that psychologically conditions us to sacrifice intimate relationships as we invest our time and talent just to get the stuff we are deceived into thinking we have to have. We like to think ourselves above the manipulation of the geniuses of Madison Avenue, but in the end we succumb to their inventions and become addicted to the products they tell us are essential to our well-being. Without advertising our democratic capitalism, this last great idea of human history, would die. It is advertising that keeps America running, and it is advertising that keeps us running too.

Do not underestimate those brainy people who pour themselves into producing the ads that interrupt soap operas and ball games. Television ads are some of the most brilliantly contrived art forms of all time. Compare the amount of money spent on producing a minute of television advertising (often in the millions of dollars) with what is spent for a minute of regular programming, and it will be easy to figure out which attracts the greatest creativity.

The unique character of advertising, in its most modern form, is that it aims at gratifying the deepest spiritual and emotional needs of its targeted audience. This is in contrast to what advertising used to do. There was a time when ads gave us information about the products, but that was when we needed what was being sold. In those days, the ads described the materials used in production, gave data about the durability of the products, and even cited technical details that would provide scientific grounds for choosing what was being advertised over the competition. But this old kind of advertising only worked because people had a need for what was up for sale.

Appealing to the Satiated Consumer

Advertising has to be far more sophisticated if it is to appeal to those of us whose basic needs have already been satiated. In our consumer-oriented society, advertising must be able to convince us to desperately want things that, for the most part, did not even exist a couple of decades ago. But those who contrive the ads have great insight into our collective psyche and have tailored their pitch to convince us that what is being sold will provide such essential requisites as security, love, status, and peace of mind.

To listen to the ads is to be assured that everything needed for spiritual well-being can be secured if we just have enough money. Hamburgers are sold by appealing to our sense of losing out on life: "You deserve a break today . . . at McDonald's." In reality all you get for your money is some ground meat.

"Buick is something you can believe in!" Here you thought a Buick was an automobile, and the ad makers tell you it's a religious conviction!

There's a big-time beer ad in which some guys are seated by a stream cooking fish over an open fire. It is eventide, and it's obvious that these sportsmen have had a good day. A deep voice sings out, "Here's to good friends. Tonight is kind of special . . ." Then one of the guys rips off a can from a six pack, tears off the tab, holds it up, and with deep sincerity says to his friends, "You know guys, it doesn't get any better than this." *We're looking at a can of beer,* but the ad conveys the idea that what comes with the beer is a sense of intimacy with good friends. This of course has a lot of appeal to those of us who are too busy to go fishing with our friends, or who are so caught up rushing around that we really don't have any friends at all. Psychologically, we are being conditioned to associate friendship with a particular brew, and our hunger for friendship is translated into a desire for a particular beer.

We certainly don't need cigarettes, but for many men whose macho feelings are being threatened by everything from the women's movement to "Donahue," the promise of becoming a Marlboro man strikes a responsive chord.

Then there's the most famous ad of all time. In it we are shown people from all the nations of the world, dressed in their native costumes. There are Serbs and Croates from Yugoslavia. There are blacks and whites from South Africa. There are people from Asia and Latin America, and ethnic types from all over Europe. They are holding hands. They are singing together in unison, "I'd like to teach the world to sing in perfect harmony . . ." And what is it that brings perfect harmony to broken humanity? It's Coca-Cola. And if there's any doubt about the validity of the claim, a strong authoritative voice assures us, "It's the *real* thing."

When Jesus attacked materialistic lifestyles it was at a time when things were fairly uncomplicated. He simply pointed out that, on the one hand, there are material things that can provide materialistic gratifications. And on the other hand, there are spiritual things that can provide spiritual gratifications. What Jesus didn't have to face was a world in which people were increasingly convinced that there are material things that will provide spiritual gratification. I wonder what He would say to people who are ready to spend money they don't have to buy things they don't need to impress people they don't know and who, in the end, are people who don't care. Would he not cry out in His ancient tongue, *"Raca!"* which means "Fools!"?

By suggesting that ads promise that consumer goods will gratify the deep psychological and spiritual hungers in our lives I do not want to communicate the idea that in such a society religion is believed to be unnecessary. Quite the opposite. God has seldom been more talked about than He is in our intensely consumer-oriented society. It's just that the function of God has been changed. He has a whole new role. No longer is He the object of all worship and adoration. Instead He has become an important means for getting what we now worship and adore—things, or at least the money to buy the things. In our brave new world, we worship the things we have been conditioned to want, and we will be religious if religion can guarantee us the products our democratic capitalistic society turns out by the tons. Our God is very much a part of this last great idea of human history.

The Church of the Consumer

In a variety of forms, a new religion is vying for allegiance, and it is winning converts left and right. It stands in diametrical opposition to biblical faith, even though it still uses the terminology of Scriptures. It is a religion that has ascribed the name of Jesus to its deity, even though there is little resemblance between the historical Jesus and the new one created in the image of a contemporary personality who reflects our cultural values. This new Jesus propagates a "prosperity theology" that promises the faithful if they seek first the kingdom of this reconstructed deity and do all the things the pop religious books say will guarantee success, then all these things (the ones described in the ads) will be added unto them. This is a new religion that is functional, fit for these new believers who hunger for consumer goods. It has, as they say, "user-friendly churches" that are just right for people whose God is a super-genie who can be at our beck and call through prayer and who will help us succeed in life . . . which of course means to get all the things we don't need, so as to gratify our media-created hungers.

From time to time, a Mother Teresa comes along and reminds us of the other Jesus. We admire her and Him. But then we hurry back to that real Jesus who doesn't demand sacrifices for the poor and the oppressed but simply promises to be there to help us to be, as the ad for the army suggests, all that we can be.

PART III

FINDING THE CURE

7

Living Out a Commitment to Creating the Kingdom of God

*T*here is an antidote to our deadness. That deadness which spreads over those of us who have been seduced into a consumeristic lifestyle can be lifted. We, who, like Sleeping Beauty, have fallen under the spell that renders us unconscious to love and joy can be awakened. It comes from the kiss of dreams and visions. It comes in the good news of what we might become in the "not yet." What we might be is where we find the essence of our faith and the promise of a new beginning. It is in our believing in a glorious future for oppressed humanity and in the roles that we can play in bringing that future to pass that we can find a meaning for our lives. It is in the vision of the kingdom of God and in God's calling for us to help make it happen that we find a resurrection from deadness and a hope for glory.

Let's get more specific. God has promised to transform this world into a world wherein His will is done, and He calls on us to pray for this world when we pray the prayer He taught us to pray:

"Our Father which art in heaven, Hallowed be thy name. Thy kingdom come. Thy will be done in earth, as it is in heaven." (Matt. 6:9–10)

But we dare not pray for something we are not committed to work for. Indeed, to be Christian is to have committed our lives to being the people God uses to build His kingdom and express His will in every sector of society and in every avenue of human endeavor. More specifically, when the vision of that kingdom inspires someone, and the dream of having a significant part in creating it becomes a realistic personal vocation, a new vitality races through the nerves and sinews.

Dreamers and Visionaries

Such an individual is Brian Stevenson, an African-American and one of my former students. During his undergraduate days Brian proved to be a notch above others. He excelled in his studies. He was a star athlete and a leader in the student government. On top of everything else, Brian was a concert pianist.

Beyond all of these accomplishments, Brian had a dream. It was to serve the oppressed. He wanted to be a lawyer and use his talents to defend people who seemed to be victimized by a system that often denied justice to those who are poor. His dream led him to apply to Harvard Law School. Again he excelled. Again he demonstrated that he had the gifts and intelligence to achieve almost anything. And again he graduated with honors.

It is hard to estimate what an African-American who graduates from Harvard Law School is able to earn. Almost any major firm in the country would have found him to be an extremely attractive candidate. Salary offers of $100,000 a year would be a conservative estimate. But today Brian is earning a mere pittance. In order to live out his dream he lives in a one-room flat in Montgomery, Alabama, and spends his days working to rescue those in prison who wait on death row. He has saved some who were not given fair trials. He makes sure that cases of condemned men and women are carefully reviewed. He does his best to make justice a reality for those who otherwise would not have it.

When I asked him about whether he believed in capital punishment, he assured me he didn't. But he went on to explain that even if he did, he would still be doing what he does. In Alabama, as in many states, he said, there is one kind of justice for rich people and for whites, and another kind for poor people, especially blacks. He sees it as his mission to struggle against this reality and to try to change things so that God's justice comes into play. He is trying to make the kingdom of God a reality, if only in a limited way, in Montgomery, Alabama.

If you were to meet Brian, you would sense a radiant aliveness about him. There is an excitement in his demeanor, and he possesses the quality that Abraham Maslow called *self-actualization*. This is what comes from being a visionary and a dreamer. These are the traits of people Jesus makes alive as they respond to His call not to be conformed to this world and to press on to the high calling of God (Phil. 3:14).

Another who lived out what he believed was his God-given vision was a man named Arthur De Moss. I first met him when I was the young pastor of a Baptist church in Bridgeport, Pennsylvania. As was my custom, at the end of my Sunday morning worship services, I gave an invitation to anyone who wanted to make a public commitment to live for Christ. Art responded; he came down the aisle to declare his desire to be in full-time Christian service. I thought by coming to the altar he was expressing his desire to leave the world of business and enter into the gospel ministry. That was not the case. He told to me he thought there were more than enough preachers in the world. What was really needed, he said, was for God to raise up some millionaires who would be willing to use their money to support missionary work.

In the years that followed, Arthur De Moss turned a little home-based company into one of the largest health-insurance companies in the country. He made millions of dollars, and true to his word, he used his money to finance missionaries and to underwrite some of the most significant evangelical organizations in Christendom.

Art died unexpectedly while still a relatively young man. Those who attended his funeral told about how remarkable it was. Person after person gave testimony of how Art had impacted their lives and how he was a person who had lived his life with passion. It could easily be said that in following Jesus, Arthur De Moss lived out the Latin admonition, *Carpe Diem*.

People like Brian Stevenson and Arthur De Moss who are committed to changing the world into the kingdom of God are visionaries. They are the kind of people who demonstrate that deadness of spirit need not be the subjective condition of those who live in this present age. Their vitality, love for life, and passionate lifestyles stand in diametrical opposition to what has become the common emotional condition of those who have bought into the last great idea of history. These are the people the prophet Isaiah spoke of when he declared:

> But they that wait upon the LORD shall renew their strength;
> they shall mount up with wings as eagles; they shall run, and
> not be weary; and they shall walk, and not faint. (Isa. 40:31)

The thing that is obvious to those of us who are privileged to know such dreamers and visionaries is how tireless they seem to be. They do so much on any given day that they make the accomplishments of others seem puny by comparison. At the end of the day others are exhausted while the strength of these kingdom builders seems renewed—just like the prophet said it would be. As these comparisons are made, it becomes painfully apparent that the tiredness of many people does not come from physical exertion but from the meaninglessness of what they do. To work for no higher goal than to get enough money to buy things that nobody really needs is not the sort of thing that feeds the soul.

Think of it! Have the people in our society ever been more stressed out and emotionally dissipated than they are today? And isn't it obvious that what lies behind the people who have been so psychically deadened by their lives in the workplace is the fact that what they are doing isn't worthy of their humanity? Is it not the case that most people appear to be caught up in what they perceive to be an almost endless grind and that they have been duped into thinking this is a requirement in life? They see no other way to live.

What furthers my sadness is the new generation coming along that seems to be even more bogged down in acquiring *things*. The majority of the young people I meet in schools and colleges across the nation have been socialized by television. And like Chauncy Gardner in Jerzy Kosinsky's book, *Being There*, they have taken on the values and the prescribed lifestyle defined by the media. They choose their vocations in light of what will yield the money they believe they need to gratify their TV-nurtured consumeristic appetites. The effects are obvious, and I feel so sad to be with them. Their resultant apathy is apparent not only to the objective observer; they themselves see it too. They will actually use the word *apathetic* to define their peers. High-school cheerleaders talk about their inability to elicit any enthusiasm from student spectators at games, regardless of what acrobatics (literally) are employed. In one school I visited, a student had scribbled on a hallway wall, "Tomorrow will be canceled because of lack of interest."

On a personal note, there is one vocation that would frighten me if I were required to get into it. That is being a church youth worker. I shudder at the thought of having to go into a group of some thirty to forty teenagers to try to elicit some kind of enthusiastic participation. To get them to sing a gospel chorus or get them to be genuinely involved in discussion would require a charisma and a talent that only a superior species might possess. I can just see myself standing in front of them, strumming my guitar and doing my best to generate some kind of enthusiastic response. A firing squad seems less threatening.

College students are much the same. Go into any classroom building, walk down the hallway, and peek into the lecture halls. You are likely to see rows of students with deadpan faces slouched in their seats. The professors can rant and rage and even make outlandish statements in a vain effort to elicit a response. Except for a possible sentence or two scribbled into a notebook, the only observable response is an upraised hand, too often followed by the question, "Do we have to know this for the final exam?"

They need visions! Both young people and adults. The present situation only lends support to the prophet's warning that unless the young have visions and the old have dreams, the people perish.

How Do You Catch a Dream?

But where do visions come from, and what is the source of dreams? How do these energizing convictions invade the human psyche, and how do these motivating hopes become part of a mind-set that makes people passionately alive?

Such a question is easy to answer in one sense, but difficult in another. Subjectively when it comes to explaining how an ordinary person gains a life-fulfilling, meaningful vision, getting an answer is an arduous task. If an individual asks, "How can I discover what God has called *me* to do with *my* life?" the answer is hard to come by. But objectively and collectively we Christians can get a clear and definite answer. The Bible calls us to work for justice and to join God in recreating the world. We are called to end oppression for all people and especially for the poor. The vision of the new society that God wants to create through us is cited throughout the Scriptures, but I find that vision particularly clear in the words of the prophet Isaiah:

For, behold, I create new heavens and a new earth: and the former shall not be remembered, nor come into mind. But be ye glad and rejoice for ever in that which I create: for, behold, I create Jerusalem a rejoicing, and her people a joy. And I will rejoice in Jerusalem, and joy in my people: and the voice of weeping shall be no more heard in her, nor the voice of crying. There shall be no more thence an infant of days, nor an old man that hath not filled his days: for the child shall die an hundred years old; but the sinner being an hundred years old shall be accursed. And they shall build houses, and inhabit them; and they shall plant vineyards, and eat the fruit of them. They shall not build, and another inhabit; they shall not plant, and another eat: for as the days of a tree are the days of my people, and mine elect shall long enjoy the work of their hands. They shall not labour in vain, nor bring forth trouble; for they are the seed of the blessed of the LORD, and their offspring with them. And it shall come to pass, that before they call, I will answer; and while they are yet speaking, I will hear. The wolf and the lamb shall feed together, and the lion shall eat straw like the bullock: and dust shall be the serpent's meat. They shall not hurt nor destroy in all my holy mountain, saith the LORD. (Isa. 65:17–25)

In this passage of Scripture, the kingdom of God is declared to have the following characteristics:

1. Infant mortality is eliminated as a social problem.

2. People get to live out their lives to old age. Life expectancy is more than one hundred years, and all of life is marked with health and happiness.

3. People gain the benefits of their own labor. Economic exploitation comes to an end. They get to live in the houses they build and get to enjoy the fruits of their own labor. Work becomes a joy to them.

4. Nature will be rescued from the effects of the Fall and restored to what God willed it to be. The pain and destruction of nature that characterize what is going on in the physical environment these days will come to an end, and the peaceable kingdom will be revealed.

These are the things we should work to make happen in our world. We should be organizing movements and challenging our churches to achieve these ends. We should be encouraging our youth to choose vocations in which they can spend their energies bringing about these kingdom values. And most important of all, the realization of this vision in human history should be our commitment as long as we live.

As we live out our lives for the kingdom of God we, ourselves, will be changed. In struggling to make peace and justice manifest in society we, ourselves, will be transformed into peacemakers who are pure in heart (Matt. 5:8–9). While working toward making society into what God wants it to be, we will find that our own personalities will be gradually reformed so we become more Christ-like.

In simple language, we are changed as we work for change. We are sanctified *in the process and through the process* of being co-laborers with God in struggling to make the kingdom of God visible on earth as it is in heaven.

Rescuing a World Gone Wrong

The vision of a future in which God's will is done "on earth as it is in heaven" is the theme around which the story of His salvation is constructed. Jesus came, died, and conquered the powers of darkness, not just to ensure us of a life of everlasting bliss after death, but primarily to reclaim a creation that He created "good" and that was shattered when humanity ushered in the demonic powers of evil. When we try to figure out what God wants us to do with our lives, there is little doubt that more than anything else He wants us to partner with Him in rescuing a world gone wrong. Nowhere is this more clear than in the words of the apostle Paul, who told us that all of creation is waiting for us to become His instruments for the renewal of nature and the restructuring of society:

> For we know that the whole creation groaneth and travaileth
> in pain together until now. (Rom. 8:22)

As far as the realm of nature is concerned, God is calling for His people to join Him in His efforts to rescue His creation from the devastating effects of careless exploitation. The last great idea of history, as

Washington think-tank scholar Francis Fukuyama calls the democratic capitalism of our new world order, has driven us to level rain forests, pollute rivers, and pump poisonous gases into the atmosphere. Almost everywhere we turn we see the detrimental effects of a *laissez faire* economic system. In our efforts to maximize profits, we have exploited our God-given environmental resources with little regard to what we will leave behind for future generations. And in our reluctance to institute necessary controls over the interests and practices of economic corporate powers, we have allowed our planet to be pushed to the edge of ecological disaster. We can only wonder, how long it will be before people of God around the world wake up to His call to vocations of environmental responsibility. For many, a sense of being part of the rescuing of a dying planet can provide a vision that can energize them with new and purposeful life.

Whenever I talk about lives committed to the rescuing of creation, I find an array of self-proclaimed "hard-nosed" Christians who contend that there are more important things to do with our lives. I try to convince them that such an attitude reflects a failure to understand the importance of nature in the economy of God. The Bible makes clear a basic truth that we self-centered humans find difficult to accept, namely, that the natural universe was not created primarily for us. There is no doubt that God wants us to enjoy it and even use its resources to optimize a good life for ourselves. But the ultimate purpose of creation was and is worship. Nature and all living things were created to glorify God. The stars and galaxies were spoken into place so that they might declare the majesty of the Lord: "The heavens declare the glory of God; and the firmament sheweth his handywork" (Ps. 19:1).

As the old hymn "This Is My Father's World" so eloquently states, all of nature was ordained to sing God's praises. The whale, which the Bible refers to as the "leviathan of the deep," was especially created to sing songs to its Creator (Ps. 104:26).

What all of this means is that those who choose to accept the challenge to "save the whales" are choosing a holy vocation. Those saints, whom some shortsighted religionists refer to as "eco-freaks," are carrying out a divine mandate. Actually, if whales were created to bring glory to God and to magnify *His* name, then to save a species of whales from extinction is to preserve a hymn of praise that would otherwise be silenced.

God is at work in the world and He *will* make all things new (Rev. 21:5). Those who see all of this as a dimension of the kingdom of God that is to come are those whose vision of the future is in tune with the biblical revelation. To spend one's life participating with God in protecting God's subhuman choir is to live out love and grace. I know such people, and I have found among them the aliveness that comes from purposeful living.

At church my wife made friends with a lovely Christian woman whose two sons had been raised in the church and taught the values of traditional evangelicalism. The children grew up, were well educated, and chose vocations that were significant and self-actualizing, at least to them.

However, their mother was not so sure. One Sunday, following a worship service where one of the boys had preached, my wife talked to this good woman and asked what her other son was doing. The mother expressed pride in the young man who had preached the sermon that day, and then, with less enthusiasm, explained that his brother was a crew member on the *Sea Shepherd*. Those who serve on this ship regularly go to sea in an all-out effort to save the whales from whalers. In peril of their lives, these heroic seafarers are more than ready to position themselves between harpoons and the sacred leviathan.

One son was in Christian ministry; he was into what we traditionally refer to as church work. The mother was as ready to proudly tell people about him as she was hesitant to talk about the son who was committed to saving the whales.

Who can blame her? One never knows how people will react to talk about the *Sea Shepherd*. But with my wife, that lady had found more than an interested party. Peggy was downright enthusiastic about it, thrilled to be talking to the mother of a crew member. My wife let it be known in no uncertain terms that she thought that saving the whales was a noble, God-given calling. She told that mother that she was a member of Greenpeace and was convinced that what this young man was doing could be his Christian ministry. Of course she was right.

8

Making Things Right for Everybody

*R*escuing nature from its oppressed condition is only the beginning of living out the vision of being kingdom of God people. The realization of that inspiring new world He is creating requires much more. Most important is joining the even greater calling of liberating oppressed people and freeing them to become all that God predestined for them before they were ever born. The kingdom of God is where people live out their lives in a way that allows them to express their gifts and talents, and where they enjoy the fulfillment that comes from using those gifts and talents to bless others. This involves standing up for African-Americans and Hispanic people and other minorities. It means trying to rid society of those drugs and alcohol addictions that sap the life out of individuals and their families.

The work of the kingdom of God requires us to be peacemakers. Where there is conflict, Christians have a commitment to stop it and work for reconciliation. Whether it's joining a "Peace for Bosnia" organization or getting involved to stop the slaughter of innocents in places like the Sudan, many Christians know that the vision that inspires them requires them to give themselves to peacemaking (see Matt. 5:19).

And there are few things that are clearer in Scripture than the directive God gives His people to end the suffering of the poor. Over and over again Jesus told those who would be His followers to be ready to do everything possible to feed the poor, clothe the naked, minister to the sick, and reach out to those without hope:

> "Then shall the righteous answer him, saying, Lord, when saw we thee an hungered, and fed thee? or thirsty, and gave thee drink? When saw we thee a stranger, and took thee in? or naked, and clothed thee? Or when saw we thee sick, or in prison, and came unto thee? And the King shall answer and say unto them, Verily I say unto you, Inasmuch as ye have done it unto one of the least of these my brethren, ye have done it unto me." (Matt. 25:37–40)

All of these ventures are but our limited attempts to participate with God in kingdom building.

Compassion Becoming a Passion

In my own family, I have watched what can happen to a person when a passion for ministry becomes a motivating force. Over the last couple of years, my wife, Peggy, has been moved to a commitment to compassion for homosexuals. That might seem strange to many Christians. But that's because many Christians have failed to take seriously our responsibility to love people—especially people who are oppressed.

In my book *20 Hot Potatoes Christians Are Afraid to Touch*, I tell the story of a friend of mine who is a pastor in Brooklyn. He is one of the most sensitive and loving men I know. He pastors a church that has seen better days. The community around the church has undergone great change, so that many of the old church members have moved away and very few new people have come in to take their places. It is a church that is struggling to stay alive.

The people of this church love my friend and try to do as well by him financially as they are able, but he still has a hard time economically. Fortunately, he is helped out by the local undertakers, who often call him to do funerals nobody else will do. When people who have no church affiliations die, somebody has to do their funerals, and my friend is one of those somebodies.

From time to time, I call this man to find out what is going on in his life. Because he serves in the place where he does, all kinds of strange and unusual things happen to him. His experiences have proved to be an invaluable source of illustrations for my books and sermons.

One day as we were talking, I asked him if anything special had happened to him the past week. He could not think of anything, so I helped him out by getting more specific. "What did you do last Tuesday morning at ten o'clock?" I inquired.

"Oh! That was an interesting morning," he responded.

"What happened to make it so interesting?" I asked.

"Well," he said, "I got a call that morning from the undertaker who has his place just down the street. He needed somebody to do a funeral and nobody else he called wanted anything to do with this one because the man had died of AIDS. I told him I'd take the funeral."

"What was it like?" I inquired.

"It was strange," he answered. "When I got to the funeral home, I found about twenty-five or thirty homosexual men waiting for me. They were in the room with the casket, just sitting as though they were frozen in their chairs. They looked as though they were statues. Each of them faced straight ahead with glassy, unfocused eyes. Their hands were folded on their laps as though some teacher had ordered them to sit that way. They almost scared me. Several of them wore the kind of clothes that made a blatant statement about who and what they were.

"I did what I was supposed to do," my friend said. "I read some Scripture and said some prayers. I made the kind of remarks that ministers make when they really don't know the dead person. After a few minutes, I ended the service and prepared to go out to the cemetery. Then I, along with those men, got into the cars that were to follow the hearse. We rode through the Holland Tunnel to the cemetery which was located near Hoboken, New Jersey. Then we all got out of the cars and went over to the edge of the grave.

"Not a word was spoken by any of the men from the beginning of the funeral until I had finished the prayers to commit the remains of the dead man to the earth. They all just stood at the edge of the grave, as motionless as they had been when they were seated in the funeral home. I said the closing prayer and the benediction, and turned to leave. Then I realized that all of those men were still standing frozen in their places, all with blank expressions on their faces. I turned and walked back to them and asked if there was anything more I could do for them. One of them spoke."

"What did he say?" I asked.

"What he said surprised me," my friend answered. "He asked me to read the Twenty-third Psalm. He said, 'When I got up this morning to come to this funeral, I was looking forward to somebody reading the Twenty-third Psalm to me. I really like that psalm, and I figured that they always read the Twenty-third Psalm.'

"I read the Twenty-third Psalm for those men," my friend said. "When I finished, a second man spoke, and he asked me to read another passage of Scripture. He wanted to hear that part of the Bible where it says that there is *nothing* that can separate us from the love of God. So I read from the eighth chapter of Romans where Paul tells us that neither death nor life, nor angels, nor principalities, nor powers, nor things present, nor things to come, nor height, nor depth, nor any other creature shall be able to separate us from the love of God, which is in Christ Jesus.

"When I read to those men that *nothing* could separate them from the love of God, I saw some signs of emotion on their faces for the first time. Then, one after the other, they made special requests for me to read favorite passages of Scripture. I stood there for almost an hour reading Scripture to those homosexual men before we went to and headed back to Brooklyn."

When I heard that story, I almost cried. Something down deep inside of me hurt. Something in my heart ached with sadness. I realized that these men my friend described were hungry for the Word of God but would never set foot inside a church. They wanted to hear the Bible, but they wanted to stay clear of Christians, and I think I know why. I think they feel that Christians despise them. And they are probably right.

Am I suggesting that Christians gloss over biblical teachings or ignore their convictions that homosexual acts are sinful? No. Nor am I suggesting that we make a case to justify homosexual behavior. What I am calling on Christians to do is reach out and show kindness and affection toward homosexuals. My wife and I do not agree on some crucial aspects of what a ministry to homosexual people entails, but we do agree that love is treating people as Jesus would treat them.

Peggy's Christian commitment is what has motivated her to reach out to the needs of homosexuals. She has come to know many gays and lesbians. She has gained empathy with them as they suffer. Their hurts have become her hurts.

The change in her has been remarkable. She is into the Scriptures daily. Whereas once I couldn't get her into any regular pattern of Bible reading and prayer, I now find that she loves these spiritual disciplines. She enjoys getting up early in the morning so she can have plenty of quality time to spend one-on-one with God. She is reading books on theology, sociology, psychology, and biology in an effort to gain a better understanding of what homosexuality is all about. The wonder of all this can only be glimpsed in contrast to her almost anti-intellectual attitude prior to becoming committed to her cause.

Peggy is more alive, interesting, intense, joyful, purposeful, and spiritual now than at any other time in her life. With her, there is no question as to whether or not she has a calling from God. Any evidence of midlife depression and anxieties in her have all but disappeared. She's on a high, and she knows it. Biblically prescribed visions and dreams do that to people.

PART IV

THE VENTURE OF FAITH

9

Beyond a Reasonable Doubt

*T*he Bible reminds me that the wisdom of this world, the rational ob-
jectivity which the world foolishly believes is the only real basis for
truth, can actually lead us *away* from God. And as it says in Romans
1:22 and 25:

> Professing themselves to be wise, they became fools. . . .
> Who changed the truth of God into a lie, and worshipped
> and served the creature rather than the Creator, who is
> blessed for ever. Amen.

As the apostle Paul makes clear to us, the philosophies of this
world can be foolishness (2 Cor. 3:19). It is not that reason is bad or
cannot be trusted. It is just that we are misled when we try to build our
relationship with God on reason alone. We must remember that the basis
of our salvation is experiencing God in a passionate, loving relationship.

The truth about God cannot be known through some sophisticated theology or through some scientific method. The truth about God is not some propositional statement or empirical data that can be learned out of a textbook and committed to memory. The truth is that God is a person, and that person is Jesus Christ. Only those who know and love Him know anything at all about God.

There is a kind of knowledge that is different from the knowledge that is gained from reason and science. This other kind of knowledge is not a contradiction to valid science or correctly developed logic; it is just different. It is a "totally other" kind of knowledge, according to the Danish philosopher Soren Kierkegaard. The Bible simply declares:

> For my thoughts are not your thoughts, neither are your ways my ways, saith the LORD. For as the heavens are higher than the earth, so are my ways higher than your ways, and my thoughts than your thoughts. (Isa. 55:8–9)

When I try to be detached and bracket my loving relationship with Christ in an attempt to analyze it objectively, I get confused.

It shouldn't be too difficult to grasp what I am trying to get at here. Consider the fact that there are two different ways I could study a painting by Van Gogh. I could ask a chemist to analyze the painting, or I could ask an art critic to do it. From these two different persons I would end up with two very different results.

The chemist would tell me about the chemical compounds that went into the oil paints van Gogh spread across the canvas. She might even provide me with a breakdown of the components of the canvas itself.

The art critic, on the other hand, would probably ignore all of the information the chemist worked so laboriously to provide. Instead, he would explain the ways van Gogh used form and color to express the subjective emotions in his heart and soul.

It is not that one form of knowledge is true and the other false. It is just that we are dealing with two different kinds of truth. The Germans would grasp all of this more easily because they have different words for each of these kinds of knowledge. What we call hard empirical science they call *Naturwissenschaften*. And the kind of knowledge and truth we find in the arts is called *Geistenwissenschaften*. Different kinds of truth are not confusing to the Germans.

Foolish but Useful

When the Bible tells us the wisdom of this world is foolishness, it is not telling us it is useless. Rather, it is telling us it is foolish to try to use the methodologies and techniques of science and the rational deductions of philosophy to explore the truth about God. The latter is a different kind of truth, and it is a truth that is only understood if we come at it in an entirely different way. Knowledge of God requires us to come with faith and love. Only those who are filled with pride about their comprehension of this world's wisdom would try to do otherwise.

It is easy to see why so many intellectuals find it difficult to become Christians. It is hard for them to set aside the status they have gained in the halls of their universities and academies. Intellectuals are used to being superiors. They are sure they know more and can comprehend things better than other people. There is usually a powerful ego trip in such a realization. When people like me come along and declare that there is another, more important kind of truth that cannot be grasped with the skills and abilities these intellectuals have always trusted, they become uncomfortable. We tell them this new kind of knowledge requires that they "trust not in their own understanding." We try to tell these people, who are often intoxicated with the superiority they feel over lesser minds, that when it comes to knowing and loving God their precious knowledge and methodologies for investigation are useless. And furthermore, we claim that trusting in their own knowledge can get in the way of the higher and different truth that leads to God.

We tell them the simplest and least-educated barbarian who comes to love Christ knows more about God than the most thoroughly educated philosophical theologian who has never surrendered to such a loving relationship with Him. It seems to add insult to injury when we suggest that the intellectual might be able to learn about God from someone who is barely literate but is passionately in touch with the living Jesus.

10

Becoming Like a Child

*Y*ou do not have to have some kind of super-intellect to let the reason and logic of our scientific society get in the way of having a vital and glory-filled relationship with God. All you have to do to get confused is to start using the scientists' methodologies for understanding truth. Their objective, rational reflection can wreak havoc with faith.

In my own life, when I lose the perspective of a lover and seek to understand my religious life as a scientific phenomenon, doubts arise on every side. When I stop and think about it, I realize that if I had been born in another place and in another time I probably would have never gotten to know the God I love so much. I am forced to admit that I probably would have been worshiping some other god. "And what would my spiritual experiences have been then?" I am prone to ask myself.

"Might I be a fanatical Muslim ready to die for Allah?

"Might I be a Buddhist monk lost in another form of inner gratification?

"Why was I born me? Why was I born to live in my here and now?" Such questions haunt me when I try to analyze my religious experience from a sociological point of view.

And finally, there is the overpowering problem of trying to figure out how I know whether all this Christian stuff is really true. I mean, what if my Christian God is only a cultural creation, and my religion is nothing more than a means society has used to strengthen its institutions? What if Nietzsche and Marx and Freud were right after all? What if God is just a psychological defense mechanism that I, along with other weak people, dreamed up in order to survive in a world full of hurts and pains? What if life is absurd and my religion nothing more than a human attempt to create some meaning out of that absurdity?

The rational approach with its intellectual detachment often leads to such questioning, which, in turn, leads, at times, to skepticism. Whenever I become objective, I lose my faith. Like Peter on the water, when I take my eyes off Jesus and look at the realities and probabilities of where I am and what I am, I sink. But as long as I am transfixed on Him, as long as I give myself over to feeling His love for me, as long as I remember to simply stop and say His name over and over again in deep and adoring tones, the darkness of the doubt is defeated.

I find nothing to be proud about when it comes to having faith. It is not a matter of intellect. I cannot reason my way to faith. My reason only makes my faith seem foolish.

Words to Light the Way

It is in the singing of hymns that I find relief from the darkness that threatens to engulf my soul from time to time. I go into the closet in the same figurative way Jesus said I should, and when I am alone I sing love songs to my Lord. I sing:

> Fairest Lord Jesus! Ruler of all nature!
> O Thou of God and man the Son,
> Thee will I cherish, Thee will I honor,
> Thou, my soul's glory, joy, and crown!

And I sing:

> My Jesus, I love Thee, I know Thou art mine;
> For Thee all the follies of sin I resign;
> My gracious Redeemer, my Savior art Thou;
> If ever I loved Thee, my Jesus, 'tis now.

And there are times when I become like a little child and sing with childlike faith:

> Oh, how I love Jesus,
> Oh, how I love Jesus,
> Oh, how I love Jesus,
> Because He first loved me.

Satan must hate those songs because he usually leaves when I sing them! Actually, loving Jesus does what rational reflection never seems able to do. Sometimes as I sing, hot tears roll down my cheeks, and as they do they seem to cleanse me. Doubts are conquered, not in philosophical logic or in theological debate, but simply in loving Jesus and in asking Him to love me. In the end it is love that casteth out fears (1 John 4:18).

11

A Passionate Faith

*D*ionysian passion, not Apollonian reason, resurrects my dead soul from the grave and gives me back my life. In the end my deliverance comes in worship rather than in listening to useful sermons.

So often we talk about worship as some kind of duty we ought to render to God. It becomes one of those things we are supposed to do on the Sabbath to keep it holy. Not enough is said about how much we need it. Theologians say we should worship because "He is worthy." But the existential self *requires* worship because it is only in passionate worship that certainty breaks loose in the consciousness. It is only in passionate worship that I hear the most seductive voice of the ages say to me, "Come, taste of me and see how good I can be" (Ps. 34:8, my paraphrase).

Alone with Jesus

When I worship, I am always alone. Even when I worship in community, I am alone. The others around me drop away from my consciousness, and in the ecstasy of worship I sense only Jesus. It is not that the others are unimportant. Quite to the contrary. They often are the essential means through which I enter this sacred aloneness. They are the ones who transport me to that place where I find only Jesus.

True worship creates for me those settings where time ceases. It has a power over me that leaves me stranded and hanging in space. At these times I feel like all that keeps me from falling are the mighty winds of the Spirit. Like a sea gull floats in air, the Holy Spirit keeps me floating in God. Everything else drops away, and I mount up like an eagle and fly.

I do not want to disparage Christian community in any way. Without this community I would have never learned of this blessed aloneness with God. I even go so far as to say that those who do not know how to be together with the people of God may never learn how to be alone with God.

Any objective, reasonable examination of the church will reveal all its flaws and show us the shortcomings and pettiness of its members. But in spite of such shortcomings and pettiness, when these flawed people get together and sing with emotion to the Jesus they love, I no longer see their failures; instead I flow and bask in the enveloping presence of the Holy Spirit they set loose around me. The new wine that fills me with new life comes in earthen vessels. The glory of the Lord I find in the church at worship is so all-consuming it makes me unconscious of the flaws in the people from whom that glory flows.

There is a time for reform. And, indeed, the church needs reforming. But that comes later. Reform comes when the worship is over and we move from subjective ecstasy to objective reflection. Once the Holy One is experienced and our hearts burn with His presence, reform is inevitable. The taste of His purity makes us want the body in which He dwells to be holy and acceptable unto God. Anything less than purity in His "now body" becomes intolerable.

When the prophet Isaiah went up into the temple to pray and was transported in worship to the very throne of God, his immediate response was an awareness of his own sinfulness and the sinfulness of the people around him. Reform and cleansing followed. In a passage that somewhat describes a spiritual transport that really cannot be expressed in words, we see the connection between what can happen in the mystical ecstasy of worship on the one hand and the reform of the people of God on the other. This famous passage sets forth the kind of glorious aloneness-in-community one can find in the throes of worship. And there is also a sense of the intensity of spiritual aliveness that worship can bring:

> In the year that king Uzziah died I saw also the Lord sitting upon a throne, high and lifted up, and his train filled the temple. Above it stood the seraphims: each one had six wings; with twain he covered his face, and with twain he covered his feet, and with twain he did fly. And one cried unto another, and said, Holy, holy, holy, is the Lord of hosts: the whole earth is full of his glory. And the posts of the door moved at the voice of him that cried, and the house was filled with smoke.
>
> Then said I, Woe is me! for I am undone; because I am a man of unclean lips, and I dwell in the midst of a people of unclean lips: for mine eyes have seen the King, the LORD of hosts. Then flew one of the seraphims unto me, having a live coal in his hand, which he had taken with the tongs from off the altar: And he laid it upon my mouth, and said, Lo, this hath touched thy lips; and thine iniquity is taken away, and thy sin purged. Also I heard the voice of the Lord, saying, Whom shall I send, and who will go for us? Then said I, Here am I; send me. (Isa. 6:1–8)

There is always a connection between social reform and the mystical excitement of being carried into the awesome presence of God. The inevitable linkage between the aliveness of loving God and a drive for personal and social purification is clearly demonstrated in the life of John Wesley. His emotional encounter with God in his conversion quickly translated itself into a social-action program that transformed England.

The American counterpart of Wesley was Charles Finney, the Billy Graham of the nineteenth century. After a conversion experience and time with God that was filled with almost unbearable joy, Finney became a primary force in the antislavery movement and a host of other social reforms, including the women's suffrage movement. Social evils became intolerable to him because of his experience with God.

And yet for all the positive consequences of mountaintop experiences with God, my best times with Him are in the ordinary, everyday pleasures of life. I feel a passionate love for God in the simple things of life. Sometimes when I am on a walk and happen upon wild rabbits or a deer I feel as Walt Whitman did, and I say to God, "I think I want to live with them. 'They do not sweat and whine about their condition. They do not lie awake in the dark and weep for their sins. Not one is dissatisfied, not one is demented with the mania of owning things.'"

Natural Joy

In the usual rounds of life, I like to think of how much God loves me, and when I do that, living with all my might seems easy to me. I want to tell jokes, not because they are funny, but because I want an excuse to laugh without seeming ridiculous to a world that demands that I have a reason for laughing. Strange as it seems, laughter comes naturally to me when I feel the closeness of God.

For me, walking with God is not a nervous carefulness of "walking circumspectly in the world," as was dictated in the covenant of the Baptist church in which I was reared. Instead, it is a time that makes me happy. And as I walk with Him and feel His goodness, I feel good too. Having God is to enjoy Him. And those who do not enjoy Him do the kingdom harm. Cold and dead saints who do not enjoy this life lead people to hell because people turn away from God when they see no joy in those who claim to walk with Him.

My prayers are not primarily petitions for help, although petitioning God for myself and for others is part of my daily life. The best part of my prayer life is the time when I share with Him how much I am enjoying things.

Once, when I was riding in a car with a rigid fundamentalist on the way to a speaking engagement, we came over the crest of a hill and there, spread out before us, was a magnificent vista of mountains and sky. I was so taken by what I saw that I said out loud, "God, that's beautiful."

My uptight religious traveling partner responded with strong disapproval. "I wish you wouldn't talk like that around me," he muttered.

He didn't even realize I wasn't talking to him. I was talking to God, and he thought I was using profanity.

12

Embracing the Feminine Side of God

*T*here is a feminine side of God. I always knew this. Even before the feminist movement demanded that I use inclusive language to publicly declare this truth, I saw this side of God in the Jesus who approached the world with what we would call a feminine sensitivity and appreciation. The way our Lord considered the lilies of the field and the way He gave pause to the smallest bird that might fall dead from a tree made me see the feminine side of God most clearly.

If the male side of God's character was expressed by Jesus' strong declarations of truth and pronouncements on morality, the female side of God was clear in His gentle sense of wonder while enjoying what the less perceptive would call the simple things of life. If I could have been around in Jesus' time, I do not think I would have so much wanted to see Him perform miracles and defy the self-righteous religionists as I would have enjoyed sneaking along after Him as He took His private walks. I would have loved peeking at Him from behind some boulder on a hillside near the Sea of Galilee and watching Him be charmed by all the sights and sounds that surrounded Him. I would have liked watching the way Jesus looked at all the people He met and seeing how he delighted Himself with simple food and the taste of water.

The Melody That He Gave to Me

The masculine side of God is something to be admired. But it is the feminine side that draws love out of me. It is this feminine side of God I find in Jesus that makes me want to sing duets with Him. When I think about the feminine in Him, I want to throw out my arms and be loved.

When I was younger and tougher and trying to be a dead serious prophet (and what young preacher doesn't have some desire to play such a role?) I was offended by a hymn that was loved by many of the elderly members of the congregation at the church I pastored. During the hymn singing in our Sunday evening services there was a time for requesting favorites, and I could count on one of them asking for "I Come to the Garden Alone." But the more I, myself, become an old guy, the more I understand why they requested that hymn. In my younger days, it seemed to reek of mushy sentimentality, and I always felt that there was some neo-Freudian lovemaking going on between some of the elderly ladies and Jesus. Maybe I was right, but in my narrow and perverted thinking, I failed to see how pure and beautiful that could be. As I give up my messianic tendencies and more and more simply surrender to the Messiah in love, this hymn becomes increasingly meaningful to me:

> I come to the garden alone,
> While the dew is still on the roses;
> And the voice I hear, falling on my ear;
> The Son of God discloses.
>
> He speaks, and the sound of His voice
> Is so sweet the birds hush their singing,
> And the melody that He gave to me,
> Within my heart is ringing.

I'd stay in the garden with Him
Though the night around me be falling,
But He bids me go; through the voice of woe,
His voice to me is calling.

And He walks with me, and He talks with me,
And He tells me I am His own;
And the joy we share as we tarry there,
None other has ever known.

In my youth I wanted to be like Martin Luther King, but the older I get, the more my role model becomes Saint Francis of Assisi. Of course there was a lot of Saint Francis in Dr. King and a lot of Dr. King in Saint Francis. But now it is the loving of Jesus in the Spirit that is becoming more and more a preoccupation of my life.

Recognizing the Feminine Side of Myself

Not only do I love the feminine in Jesus, but the more I know Jesus, the more I realize that Jesus loves the feminine in me. In a day and age when so many women are trying to rediscover the side of their humanity that the world deems masculine, I find Jesus is helping me to appreciate those dimensions of me the world calls feminine.

I find myself wanting to be the bride of Christ. I want Him to find in me, or, if need be, to *create* in me, a sweetness and a sensitivity for all things and all people. I want more and more for Him to find in me, or to create in me, a gentle heart and an awareness of the goodness that lies in people around me and especially in my enemies.

Once I wanted to be the enemy of the enemies of Jesus. But little by little I am realizing that Jesus refuses to declare any of us to be His enemies, even though there are those who would like to dignify themselves by assuming the title. And the more I become aware that our Lord does not view His enemies as His enemies, the more it becomes difficult for me to define them as my enemies.

I want to learn to love those people who stand on the other side of the struggles in which I am engaged. I pray that Jesus will bring out in me that blessed trait, which some disparage as feminine weakness, that will enable me to find the good in the racist, the homophobe, the fascist, and the militarist. The side of me that the world calls masculine would want them destroyed. But as Jesus draws out the feminine in me, He makes me want to see them rescued by having the goodness that is in them overcome the evil.

There is that feminine side of me that must be recovered and strengthened if I am to be like Christ. And it is in the recovering of that side of my humanity that I find myself more and more willing and less and less afraid to be called "a bride of Christ."

Society has brought me up to suppress the so-called feminine dimensions of my humanness. But when Jesus makes me whole, both sides of who I am meant to be will be fully realized. Then, and only then, will I be fully able to love Jesus and be fully able to accept His love for me. Until I accept the feminine in my humanness, there will be a part of me that cannot receive the Lord's love. And until I feel the feminine in Jesus, there is a part of Him with which I cannot identify. What I long for in the end is to know the way He can love Himself through me and I can love myself through Him. Only when I know Him in His wholeness and am myself made whole will this happen. And when it does happen, I will be fully alive in Him and He in me. It is not yet, but it will be. And this is the good news:

> Beloved, now are we the sons of God, and it doth not yet appear what we shall be: but we know that, when he shall appear, we shall be like him; for we shall see him as he is. (1 John 3:2)

PART V

DECIDING ON A CALLING

13

Having Dreams and Visions

A calling must be personal. This means the most troubling question most individuals have to struggle with is how to discover God's *specific* will for their lives.

It is all good and well to talk about God's will for history and the *Shalom* that He wants all humanity to know and share. But such wonderful visions of a world that ought to be are far too general for most of us. A Christian usually wants to know in a clear and direct fashion what God expects of him or her. The most common question we hear from a person who wants to love God with heart and mind and strength is, "How do I figure out what God wants me to do with my life?" It is one thing to talk about His will for history and to describe what will be the nature of things when His kingdom comes on earth as it is in heaven. But something more "role specific" is what is being sought here.

What Should I Be Doing?

This question is often spelled out in vocational terms. "As I work for the kingdom of God," the Christian asks, "just what is it I am supposed to be doing?"

Business people struggle with this question, and it leads some of them to drop out and go to seminary. College seniors who realize that the possibility of evading the making of a vocational choice is coming to an end may become panic-stricken trying to figure out what God is calling them to do next. Homemakers wonder whether they are called to do things that some shortsighted people might consider to be more significant. The question is everywhere, and even when it is asked in nonreligious terms, its urgency is difficult to miss.

What makes this question even more difficult to answer is that often Christians have a hard time believing what God wants them to do is something they would *enjoy* doing. Time and time again I hear my students say they are not sure if it's "the flesh" or the Lord motivating them to choose what seem to be inviting vocational options. It is almost as though they believe that if it looks like fun it can't be right.

This is not to suggest there is not some validity to such questioning. Anyone who has ever had to interview possible recruits for missionary work is well aware that there are many who, in temporary bursts of emotion, romanticize what they think they want to do with their lives. The desire to do something heroic and admirable can easily lead a young person to claim a readiness to go to some place like Haiti or the Sudan to serve for a lifetime. Unfortunately, once many of these unrealistic teenagers go to serve in such difficult places they quickly come to terms with some hard truths. As soon as the initial excitement wears off and the effects of culture shock begin to be felt, such young women and men start looking for a quick way out. They usually find it.

More than half of those who go to the mission field fail to serve more than two years. The enormous waste and poor stewardship are obvious when one considers the financial resources that are required to place a Christian worker in another country and the fact that unfamiliarity with language and culture usually severely limit what can be accomplished in the first couple of years on the field.

When I say that missionary work can serve to meet romantic ideals, I mean that in just about every way. In the dating game, a very ordinary guy often figures out he can become a superstar with the young women in his church youth group just by announcing that he feels called to "full-time missionary service." Convinced that she doesn't want to marry an ordinary guy but wants to be with a man who will be some kind of spiritual giant, a young woman may get starry-eyed about the guy who declares himself to be a missionary candidate. It's all quite sexist in that it assumes a woman is going to have her role in life defined by whom she marries, but that's the way it often is. Having been the executive director of a missionary organization for more than a quarter of a century, I know these cases all too well.

Anything Can Happen

Even as I describe those who are confused about the call to missionary work, I don't want to appear cynical. I am still ready to affirm the dreams of dreamers and undergird those who are, in the words of William Carey, ready to "attempt great things for God, and expect great things from God." If there is anything I want to avoid, it is being the crusher of dreams and visions. I have seen others do that sort of thing, and it is an ugly thing to behold.

I watched once as some dreams got crushed for a group of inner-city kids from "the projects." In many cities the projects are the low-cost communities owned and run by the housing authority. The projects often show the effects of years of neglect, and the people who live in them tend to be the most disadvantaged and despondent of the city. These places are filled with single-parent African-American and Hispanic families who, for the most part, live off the welfare system.

In this case the teenagers lived in the Philadelphia projects. Usually teenagers from these projects drop out of school and just hang out on street corners. The girls get pregnant, and the boys usually can be counted on to mess up and spend time in jail. This is true for most of them, except for those who get involved in our youth program. Our missionary organization, which for years has carried on educational and medical work in the Third World, has initiated a variety of inner city missionary ventures. We've come to realize you don't have to go to the Third World in order to go to the Third World anymore. You can go to the projects. We have established an array of programs ranging from tutoring to Bible study clubs.

One year we had a basketball program. Typically, kids who live in the projects love to play basketball, and getting them organized into a league took little effort. To give our kids a special thrill, I came up with the idea that an all-star team from our inner-city league might play an exhibition game with some of the Philadelphia Eagles. The Eagles are the professional football team in our city, and during their off-season, one way the players stay in shape is by playing basketball. Obviously such excellent athletes are quite capable of playing very good basketball.

When I told our kids I had set up the game, they went wild with excitement. They couldn't believe it. I set up the game to be played in the gym at Eastern College, where I teach, and made sure that a good crowd filled the bleachers the night of the big event. I had special T-shirts made up for our all-star team that read, "The Warriors."

On the night of the game I got the kids together for a special pep talk. I told them they should get a good feel for what it's like to play on a college court, because if they wanted to go to college, we would do our best to help them get there. I told them about the kind of financial aid I could get for them if they would just get their grades up.

The kids were intensely attentive. I knew they were dreaming dreams of greatness and saw for themselves promising possibilities. Suddenly, I was interrupted by the harsh voice of the coach of the team.

He was a man who had grown up in the projects and had volunteers to work with us. I had known him for years and he always seemed like a happy-go-lucky guy. That is why the anger in his voice surprised me.

"Don't listen to him!" he shouted. "Guys like him are always coming along and promising you they can get you out of the projects. Don't listen! People like him used to tell me the same thing. I tried and tried, and it didn't do me any good.

"Look at me! I'm still there, ain't I? And you're gonna be there when you're my age. So you better get used to being in the projects, and don't pay any attention to what he says."

There was dead silence following that outburst. The kids just sat there with hanging heads. I was momentarily stunned into silence by the hostility of the coach's voice. But I quickly recovered. And then with sharp and loaded words I reacted and said, "No! Don't you listen to *him*!" Then I went on to recite a poem by Shel Silverstein:

LISTEN TO THE MUSTN'TS

Listen to the MUSTN'TS, child,
Listen to the DON'TS
Listen to the SHOULDN'TS
THE IMPOSSIBLES, the WON'TS
Listen to the NEVER HAVES
Then listen close to me—
Anything can happen, child,
ANYTHING can be.

The kids all looked straight into my eyes, and I said, "OK! Now let's play some ball."

That coach had been hurt. His dreams were all faded and just about forgotten. It's painful when dreams get lost, but his pain didn't give him the right to keep those kids from dreaming. No matter what had happened to him, he had no right to puncture the hopes of some starry-eyed kids. Without dreams, kids die.

The Need for Dreams

Without personal dreams about the future, we are all dead. When we can't believe that what we dream about being and doing with our lives has any chance of becoming reality, we settle into a routinized lifestyle devoid of joy.

In the classic movie *The Graduate*, Benjamin, the main character, has an affair with Mrs. Robinson, an attractive woman who is old enough to be his mother. After weeks of bedding down with her, he attempts to get to know her as a person. As he tries to get her involved in conversation she is reluctant, but he pleads and finally she gives in and asks what he wants to talk about. Benjamin tells her he wants to talk about art. After some vain attempts to get some kind of discussion going, she finally tells him there really aren't any art styles that interest her anymore.

Benjamin tries to change the subject by asking, "Where did you and Mr. Robinson meet?"

"In college," she tells him. "He was a medical student and I was in my second year when I got pregnant, and we got married."

"What were you studying in college?" he asks.

"Art," is her response.

Every time I hear Paul Simon sing, "Hello, Mrs. Robinson," I think of the woman who lost interest in life because she had lost her dreams and her only escape was in sexual affairs with young men she hardly knew.

It is a tragedy when dreams die. When that happens, we feel a deadness in our hearts and a dryness in our souls.

In contrast to the Mrs. Robinsons of the world, there are dreamers and visionaries who live out their callings by the grace and through the power of God. The history of the church is filled with them, and they are central figures in the Bible. There's a short list of such dreamers in the eleventh chapter of the epistle to the Hebrews, and they are more than worth the time it takes to consider them. For example there is Noah, who, in the face of an evil world about to be destroyed by a flood, dreamed of something better to come. There is Abraham, who believed in a future God had promised him, even when logic gave him no grounds for believing. And then there is Moses, who rejected all the social advantages he might have enjoyed as the adopted son of Pharaoh's daughter in order to follow the leading of God. The list goes on and on, citing an array of ancient saints who lived out their God-given dreams and visions against seemingly insurmountable odds.

But where did these special people get their visions, which they, through faith, lived out? Where did they get that sense of what they were supposed to do and be? And did they discern some pattern for tuning into a call from God that we can replicate so that we, living centuries later, can be like them?

I think in most cases what worked for those ancient mothers and fathers of our faith would not work for us. If God spoke to us in a dream, most of us, in all likelihood, would discount what He had to say. One of the consequences of having a modern world view is that we treat dreams as creations of our own subconscious rather than as revelations from outside of us. We treat any inclinations of "oughtness" as hunches; only the mystically oriented among us would think of treating them as directives from God. I am not suggesting that God does not speak to us today in dreams and through "promptings in our hearts"; I am only saying that, because of being socialized into modern life, we have learned to be suspicious of such things.

Abraham at Breakfast

When it comes to deciding what we should do with our lives, most of us look for revelations through more mundane means. We seek supernatural insights through what seem to us to be rational processes. In prayerful reflection and Bible study we try to discern some guidance for the directions our lives should take.

We sometimes ask friends to help us through their good counsel. Other times we try to get some input from spiritual mentors. But in the end we feel forced to make the decisions that determine our destinies without the kind of absolute assurance we would like to have and think we ought to have.

Sometimes we are inclined to wonder what it might be like to have had the kind of clear and certain knowledge of the will of God those wonderful Bible characters seemed to possess. But stop and think again. Were those Bible people really all that sure of themselves?

Were the likes of Abraham, Joseph, and Samuel, to whom God spoke in visions and dreams, any more positive about the revelations they received than we are when we gain our visions and dreams through other means?

Did they suffer none of the anxieties that we feel when we are about to take our leaps of faith? Did they have a greater certainty about the revelations that came to them while they slept than we can have from what we conclude after meditation, Bible study, receiving input from other Christians, and prayer? Or were those Bible people just like us? Did they, as we do, have to work out their own salvation with fear and trembling (Phil. 2:12)?

Soren Kierkegaard, the Danish theologian/philosopher, gets us to use our imagination when thinking about the men and women in the Bible. Consider how he gets us to identify with Abraham. Kierkegaard asks us to imagine what it must have been like for Abraham to come to breakfast the morning after the dream in which God instructed him to offer up his son Isaac as a sacrifice to God.

Killing his son would mean the logical end to the possibility that his "seed" would create the new nation that was to be a special people of God. It must have seemed to Abraham that what he was told in the dream could not possibly have come from God since it would lead to the apparent end of everything God had promised him and his wife, Sarah. Furthermore, what was being required of him through the dream would be contrary to all moral laws. Surely a good God would not order a man to kill his own son, especially when that son, Isaac, was such an obedient and good child!

Kierkegaard gets us to wonder whether or not the thought had occurred to Abraham that the horrible dream was from something he ate. Maybe it was a case of indigestion. And maybe it was even worse than that. Maybe the dream was demonically inspired. Kierkegaard asks us to consider what anxieties Abraham may have had as he wondered whether he could trust the revelations or be sure that the voice he heard was the voice of God.

When seen in this context, the offering of Isaac is made to appear even more extraordinary than a simple first reading of this Bible story might suggest.

But Abraham did it! He acted! As did Noah and Moses and Gideon and Barak and those other people of faith!

In this day and at this time we, too, are called upon to act. We, too, are called to live out dreams and to follow visions. Like those saints of old, we are required to make some leaps of faith, to daringly step out and attempt the great, and sometimes seemingly terrible, things we believe God has called us to do. We cannot wait for certainty and the assurance that everything will work out like we would like it to. We must take risks if we are to live out our dreams. We must be ready to bet our lives on visions. And even if we appear to others to be like Don Quixote, we must dream the impossible dream. One thing is certain: If we fail to live out our dreams and visions, we perish (see Proverbs 29:18).

14

Daring to Go for It!

*M*ost of the time most of us do not have what it takes to make decisions. We are far too rational. We weigh things too much. We measure
the possible results of the alternatives and always find enough to scare
us out of making any choice at all. There are risks that go with decision-
making, and risks are too hard for those of us who <u>think too much</u>.

The really important decisions, unfortunately, have to be made
without certainty. If we get married, we do it without the certainty that
we are making the right decision. If we have children, we have them
without knowing how they will turn out. If we decide to be Christians,
we have to do it on faith, sometimes fighting a nagging sense that we
have been duped.

Only *after* decisions are made do we have any sense as to whether
we have chosen as we should. And even when we have convinced ourselves that our decisions were the right ones, we may have times of

doubt and wonder what might have been had we chosen otherwise. Inaction or the refusal to decide doesn't provide any escape from the tensions we face when decisions have to be made. For we all know that not to decide is to decide. Not to decide is to let time decide for us. For instance, if I am still standing outside the station, trying to decide whether to take the twelve o'clock train, at one minute after twelve I will have made a decision.

The Most Important Decision

Of all the decisions any of us have to make, perhaps the most important is what we choose to become. To act as though that decision has already been made and is written down in some book kept by God, as the followers of Islam do, is to abdicate one's responsibility as a human being and to practice what the French existentialist philosopher Jean Paul Sartre calls "bad faith." Sartre contends that putting the obligation to make the decisions that define the meaning and purpose of our lives onto some transcendental "totally-other-being-in-the-sky" is to reduce ourselves to puppets.

Of course it would be easier for us that way. In a sense we might all be a bit relieved to find ourselves freed from the responsibility of decision-making that goes with being human. Friedrich Nietzsche once wrote that if there were no God we would have to invent one, simply to have someone to blame for the decisions we lacked the courage to make because we didn't want to accept the responsibility of determining our own destinies.

I find that most Christians, especially the young people I meet out on the speaking circuit, are particularly keen to have a God who worked out a plan for each of their lives before they were ever born. Such plans would relieve them, as individuals, from having to work out their own salvation "with fear and trembling," as the Bible tells them to do. The fact that the Bible nowhere suggests that an overall divinely constructed plan for their lives will ever be made available to them does not keep them from expecting special revelations providing just that. Over and over again I am confronted with young people who ask me in a pleading voice, "Tony, how can I discover God's will for my life?" These people have been led to believe their destiny has already been designed and all they have to do is submit to this grand design. Then, and only then, they feel the will to be able to live lives pleasing to God.

How Do We Decide?

The biggest problem with this approach is that it tends to immobilize well-meaning Christians. Very seldom does God directly communicate any specific directions to Christians or tell them exactly what He wants them to do. I must admit that from time to time there are people who claim to have special visitations from God that define their callings for life. But such visitations are few and far between, leaving the rest of the questing Christian community wondering how they are ever going to live out the will of God for their lives when God hasn't given them a clue as to what His plans for them are all about.

Adding to the misery of these good, confused people is the claim of most ministers they hear on Sundays that *they* had some kind of special calling from the Lord. As a matter of fact, a lot of seminaries won't even consider candidates for the gospel ministry unless they can give evidence of such a call. Now far be it from me to question anybody who has had a special and specific communication from God, but it is important for me to note that some of the greatest preachers of the church (i.e., Charles H. Spurgeon) claim never to have had a specific call to the gospel ministry. They were simply people who had some talents they were ready to use in the work of the church and in the task of spreading the gospel.

I am not in the camp of the existentialist philosophers who believe that each individual is left in aloneness to create his or her own meaning for life. On the other hand, I'm not of that fond persuasion that God dictates to every sincere, seeking Christian some specific plan laid down before the foundation of the earth. Rather, I hold that what happens to most of us is that God comes alongside us and walks with us each step of life's way. Furthermore, I believe we Christians and the Lord must work out between us on each step of life's way what we ought to do and who we should be. God does not impose His plans on us but does invite us into a relationship with Him in which we are able to figure out what our lives should be about. In this relationship we will find ourselves repenting of mistakes we have made in the past, exploring new options for the future, and trying to sense if we are where we ought to be in the present.

In short, I find that life for most of us is a constant struggle in which we never stop considering what it is we should become. In dialogue with God we need to establish what we believe are viable missions and then set out to realize them. But each step along the way we must be ready to let go of the plans that have given our lives direction and accept new challenges that may grow out of the dialogue. I believe we must live on tiptoe, never sure of what the future holds, but having committed our lives to the One who will go with us into that future. We must be constantly into the Scripture and into prayer, which are essential disciplines for developing a sensitivity to the presence of God in our everyday lives.

I personally find that spending some time each day in the four Gospels is absolutely essential as I seek to let the mind of Christ permeate my heart and mind. I also find that I must regularly meet with trusted Christian friends and use them as a sounding board for what I am thinking as I try to consider those decisions I should be making. I really trust my friends to be "priests" for me, and I believe that one of the ways God comes to me is through them. Finally, I have to ask God to help me think clearly and sensibly lest I end up doing something stupid.

The good news is that even if I do end up making some stupid decision, I know it's not the end of the world for me. I live by grace. That means the Jesus I walk with day by day does not condemn me for wrong moves in my Christian walk. That's why I like Romans 8:1 so much:

There is therefore now no condemnation to them which are in Christ Jesus, who walk not after the flesh, but after the Spirit.

God is a God of new beginnings, and He *never* leaves me with the sense that I have blown everything or that it's too late to try anything new.

Such an approach to life may, at first, seem too full of questions and uncertainties for a lot of people. To me, it is an approach to life that makes my daily walk a daring adventure. Who would want a road map for life when one can set out like Abraham did when he gave his life to God and left the Ur of the Chaldees "not knowing where he was going"? Who would want to know the end when there is the invitation to yield to a presence while I feel my way through the dangerous labyrinth of life?

I suppose I want to be like the young and daring Luke Skywalker in the movie *Star Wars*, who, upon yielding to "the force," trusts his feelings and instincts about what to do. The difference for me, of course, is that "the force" is a person with a name—Jesus Christ the Lord.

In the end, I have to admit that what I decide is built on a *feeling*. When the decisions seem momentous, the feeling is deep and passionate. I listen; I pray. But in the end I act with fear and trembling. There is the excitement of the dare and the thrill of stepping out of a boat into a sea that might swallow me up. But I embrace it all with a passion and say thank you to a God who, by His grace, invites me to live dangerously.

It is a feeling! And in the end, what I get from prayer is a feeling. I long for a sense of *oughtness*, but when the chips are down I am ready to bet my life that what is to be attempted will be a great thing for God even though it may hardly be noticed by other people. In those most difficult of decision times, I do not even *talk* to God in prayer. I listen! And God does not speak to me. He *listens!* Yet in the mutuality of shared silence, I both hear and act. If you don't know what I'm talking about, I don't think I can explain it, except to assure you that such times can come like an oasis in the midst of the dry desert of doubt. And let me assure you, this way of living is never boring.

Amen!

How Will We Know God's Will?

Allow me to tell you about a friend I got to know through the Bible. His name is Jonathan. He was the princely son of King Saul and the best friend of the great David.

In 1 Samuel 14 we read a fantastic story about Jonathan and a great victory he won over the enemies of Israel, the Philistines. We learn from the Scriptures that the Philistines had been able to almost completely disarm the soldiers of Israel, leaving them with only two swords. Saul had one, and Jonathan had the other.

The warriors of Israel were being constantly humiliated by the Philistines, who stood on a nearby hill, hurling insults and challenges at them. The Philistines knew full well that the Israelites did not have the means to respond to their gibes, so they just went on like mean school boys shouting down their gibes. We read in the Scriptures how the army of Israel gathered around Saul, who was waiting with the priest who wore the ephod, that special part of the high priest's regalia that was supposed to give the wearer the ability to discern the will of God.

While Saul and his soldiers were trying to get a clear and specific word from the Lord, Jonathan and his sword bearer stood off to the side. Jonathan had had it with the Philistines' talk. He said to his sword bearer, "Let's go up and get those guys."

When the sword bearer wanted to know whether they would be in God's will and therefore assured of victory, Jonathan told him, "Let's find out. We'll go up and get those suckers, and we'll even tell them we're coming. If we beat them in battle, we'll know it was God's will, and if we're not in God's will I guess we'll die."

I like that attitude. There comes a point where a guy has got to do something and not just stand around with some ephod waiting to figure out for sure what is supposed to be done. The stakes are high, but so what? You've got to take a shot at it. In the midst of all the talk, somebody has just got to go for it.

In Jonathan's case the result was a mighty victory and the scattering of the Philistine army. Things don't always work out that great. But passionate action for God sure beats the indecisiveness that has the people of God standing around doing nothing while the chance for victory slips away.

I say here's to Jonathan, a guy who had the guts to say, "*Carpe Diem!*"

PART VI

COMING ALIVE TO GOD

15

Knowing How to Love Him

*W*hen they asked Jesus which was the greatest commandment of them all, he unhesitatingly answered:

> "Thou shalt love the Lord thy God with all thy heart, and with all thy soul, and with all thy mind." (Matt. 22:37)

The most common way to look at this passage is to recognize that it precisely defines various ways for loving God. First, we are called to love God with our minds. Being Christian is not an excuse for intellectual laziness. Being Christian requires the full exercise of our thinking abilities. As much as we are capable, we are required to think through the teachings of Jesus so we can figure out how they apply to the way we live out our own Christian discipleship. Indeed, Jesus calls us to learn about Him to this end (Matt. 11:29). We are called by Scripture to study to show ourselves "approved unto God" by becoming the kind of people who do not have to be embarrassed by lack of knowledge as we expound God's message to a skeptical world (2 Tim. 2:15). The apostle Paul further calls upon us to "have a reason for the faith that lies within us" (1 Pet. 3:15).

Heart and Soul and Strength

In this greatest commandment Jesus also requires us to love God with our souls. To the ancients, the soul was considered the seat of the will. What this means is that we are expected to lend our wills to the task of being Christian. We are being asked to *will* to do the will of God. In any given situation, each of us is to be committed to being willing to do what Jesus would do if He were in our place. Loving God requires decision-making day in and day out, because life constantly presents us with strange temptations and challenges. There are the constant temptations to give in to sexual desires in ways that would hurt people who are near and dear to us. There are the inclinations to resolve personal conflicts or to get out of difficult relational problems by lying. And there are the constant tendencies to play power games with people and to seek the psychic gratification that comes from domination. Deciding to do the right thing time and time again is an essential part of expressing our love to God, who requires our obedience above all else (John 14:21).

The *heart* is also brought into play when we give ourselves over to loving God. We are expected, in the words of Scripture, to set our hearts on the things that would please Him and to wean ourselves away from affection for "the things that are in the world" (1 John 2:15). The things of this world are varied. For some people, sports is the problem; they have made sports idolatrous. Other people are hooked on soap operas. And some people have made making money the most important thing in their lives. Jesus said:

"No servant can serve two masters: for either he will hate the one, and love the other; or else he will hold to the one, and despise the other. Ye cannot serve God and mammon." (Luke 16:13)

Finally, this verse calls us to love God with all of our *strength*. The God of the Bible affirms the physical side of our existence. To neglect our bodies, as so many Christians do, is a violation of the laws of good spiritual formation. The physically fit have their bodies in subjection and as a result tiredness rarely interferes with their devotion to God and with their happy relationships with others.

Passionate Love for the Father

Such explanations of Matthew 22:37 are good, but I believe there is more to this verse. I believe Jesus is not so much outlining here what is involved in loving God as He is describing the kind of *intensity* that should be evident in our love for God. He is talking about passion here. He is telling us to love God with everything we are. According to Jesus, every part of who we are and what we are is to be strained through our love for God. We can have a brilliant theology, a biblically prescribed lifestyle lived out with strict consistency, a well-balanced value system, and be emotionally healthy in every way, but still be a disappointment to God. What God is looking for are people whose love for Him is so intensely passionate that its only analogy here on earth is what goes on between young lovers who burn with desire for each other and who embarrass those around them by their inability to control themselves in public.

In the second chapter of the book of Revelation, we read about the church of Ephesus. Jesus had wonderful things to say about the people of this church:

"I know thy works, and thy labour, and thy patience, and how thou canst not bear them which are evil: and how thou hast tried them which say they are apostles, and are not, and hast found them liars: And hast borne, and hast patience, and for my name's sake hast laboured, and hast not fainted." (Rev. 2:2–3)

But He was still disappointed in them. He said:

"Nevertheless I have somewhat against thee, because thou hast left thy first love." (Rev. 2:4)

Passion is of ultimate importance to God.

Legend has it that when Sidharthra was a boy, he showed a keen interest in knowing about God. He asked everyone and anyone whom he thought could help him to give him instruction. Eventually, he heard of a special guru who lived alone, high in the mountains. It was said that this guru knew about the things of God more than any other teacher or prophet.

Having learned of this great and wonderful guru, Sidharthra went to find him, and when he did he asked the simple question, "How can I find God?"

The guru did not immediately answer. Instead, he asked the young Sidharthra to follow him. He led the boy to the edge of the lake, and then, unexpectedly and violently, grabbed the head of Sidharthra and shoved it under the water.

Sidharthra tried to escape the iron hold of the guru, but to no avail. Even when the strength that comes from the panic of drowning set in, he could not break the guru's hold.

Just when it seemed as though his lungs would burst and his life would end, the guru pulled Sidharthra's head out of the water. The boy gasped to regain his breath. And just as he was about to cry out against the guru for what he had done to him, the guru raised his hand to silence him. Then he said softly to Sidharthra, "When you want God as much as you have just wanted breath, you will find Him!"

There must be a hungering and thirsting after God. A casual acknowledging of His existence will not do. He is a jealous God and requires passionate devotion in worship. Going through the rituals in a mechanical manner offends Him (Amos 5:21). He is the lover of our souls. A detached theological analysis of His nature leaves Him longing for something deeper. What He desires is a psalmist-like yearning in us. He looks for prayers that sound like this:

As the hart panteth after the water brooks, so panteth
my soul after thee, O God. (Ps. 42:1)

Jesus modeled the ultimate passion for God in the Garden of
Gethsemane. The intensity of His prayerful intimacy with His Father
evidenced itself when beads of blood oozed from the pores of His brow.
There was so much psychic pressure as He focused Himself on His Father that He literally sweat blood. The total being of Jesus was riveted
on the Father. He so poured Himself out in prayer that He was emptied
of all but love. Jesus did not come out of that garden singing "Sweet Hour
of Prayer." He came out exhausted from His passionate lovemaking
with the One to whom He had pledged total obedience.

Two Obstacles to Passionate Love

If we are to know anything of what it is like to so passionately love
God, we have to change. We tend to be far too diffused and our spirits
far too dissipated to love like Jesus loved and to give ourselves like He
gave Himself to the Father. The two primary causes for this diffusion
of attention and dissipation of passion lie in our guilt and anxiety.
Unless we are free from these two demonically contrived evil spirits, we
will never be free to discover the realization of our humanness in love
for God.

Guilt is what keeps us focused on the past. As long as sin is part
of our conscious memory, it creates a fear that haunts us and renders us
weak. Guilt exhausts our psychic capacity for the passionate appreciation of anything, especially of God. It saps any spiritual aliveness from
our lives. In Nathaniel Hawthorne's *The Scarlet Letter*, a young Puritan
pastor becomes sexually involved with a woman from his congregation.
As the story unfolds, we find that the adulterous clergyman is able, for
the most part, to keep what has happened a secret. But the guilt of it
diminishes his ability to preach with passion. The fear of being publicly
exposed makes him a captive to mediocrity, and the brilliance that
once marked his fiery messages all but disappears. He loses his concentration and finds that the tiredness that comes from sleepless nights

renders him listless. It is not until he confesses his sin and finds the release that such confession brings that he is able to recover the passion and zeal for God that had formerly marked his ministry.

Conscious guilt is one thing and unconscious guilt is another. Psychologists tell us that awareness of the sin and guilt in our lives is a prerequisite to mental health. Unfortunately, most of us handle the sin in our lives by repressing it. We push the awareness of what we have done into the subconscious. Our guilt is dealt with by trying to get on with our lives as though nothing has happened, especially if we seem to have gotten away with our sin. We simply try to "forget" it—at least consciously. And after a while, we find it just doesn't seem to bother us very much. It really amazes me when I consider the things, even the terrible things, in my own life that I have been able to consciously forget and believe will not bother me any more.

In the film *Crimes and Misdemeanors*, a socially prominent man's career and reputation are threatened when the woman with whom he has been having an affair demands more of him than he can give. She refuses to go on living in the shadows of his life and tells him that unless he divorces his wife and marries her, she will go public.

The man tells his brother about his plight, and the brother arranges to have the woman killed. At first the crime is too hideous a reality to live with. The man confesses that right after the murder he found life painfully unbearable. The burden of what he caused to happen sapped the joy out of life, and he didn't know how he was going to be able to go on and face the future. But then, as he explains to a casual acquaintance over a cocktail, he gradually got over it. He admitted that as time went by, the murder bothered him less and less and that on most days he hardly thought about it at all. He was convinced that in time it just would completely stop bothering him.

Of course the man was wrong. Guilt doesn't just go away. Even when the memories of our sins are pushed into the subconscious, the sin still affects us. What has been repressed still generates a sadness. It dampens our spirits. We feel depressed. A pall of despondency hangs over us because of these repressed memories of sin. And what makes matters worse is that because of this psychological repression of sin, we do not even know *why* we are depressed. We have forgotten the sins that generate the guilt. The cause of our emotional malady has been pushed so far back into our subconscious mind that we don't realize what it is doing to us.

I do not want to create the illusion that all emotional depression is caused by the repression of the consciousness of sin. Modern scientific research provides ample evidence that clinical depression (Sigmund Freud called it *melancholia*) is often the result of biophysical factors. In many cases psychoneurotic despondency is caused by chemical imbalances in the blood and can best be treated by prescription drugs. But it is also safe to say that for some people the cause of depression really is repressed consciousness of sin.

Freud once said that what we repress by day comes out in our dreams by night. In the end, said this founder of modern psychology, we never really forget anything. What we Christians call sin is often pushed into the far recesses of our memories so we think we have forgotten it. But in the end it always comes back to haunt us. It creates self-contempt and depression. The result of this self-contempt and depression is even more difficult for us to handle because we do not recognize its source.

How often have you talked with a person who has said something like this? "I don't know what's wrong with me. I've gotten everything I ever wanted. I have a wonderful marriage, lovely children, and more money than I ever dreamed I would have. And yet I'm not happy. There's no joy to my life. There's a sadness about me. I'm so depressed it's hard for me to enjoy anything."

Such a person may have had the vitality sucked out of his or her life because of forgotten sin. Repression is taking its toll, and depression has become a prevailing cloud over all of life.

We must be freed from the sin of the past if we are to have the energy to feel passion in the present. Whether we know that sin on the conscious level, or, as I have been describing, it haunts us from the subconscious regions of our minds, the effect is a diminished capacity to experience life and to love God with any kind of a fulfilling intensity.

But for all and any who need deliverance from the effects of sin and guilt, there is incredibly good news. There is a cure! That cure is right at the core of the Christian gospel. It is the salvation of Jesus.

16

Getting Rid of the Heaviness

*J*ust recently I had the privilege (and I do mean it is a privilege) to lead a despondent person into a relationship with Christ that transformed him into a person of boundless joy. I say it was a privilege because there isn't anything I know that gives a greater sense of meaning and significance to my own life than leading another person into a salvation experience with Christ.

It all took place during a flight between Philadelphia and Denver. The man sitting next to me on the airplane had a very noticeable, strange sadness about him. It took no special sensitivity to pick up on his depression. He looked like a man who had forgotten how to laugh.

As the plane took off, I found myself asking him if there was anything I could do to help. It was one of those times when I sensed myself being led to say things that, once they are said, leave me surprised and wondering why I said them.

The man answered, "To tell the truth, I'm so down I almost wish I were dead." He began to tell me about himself and what he was feeling. He told me how he had even lost his capacity to feel anything for his wife and kids. As the conversation progressed, I realized this man had deeper problems than I was able to handle. So I told him about a friend of mine who lived close to his home and who was an outstanding therapist and counselor. I was able to convince him to seek help by going to see my friend.

A few weeks later, I got a telephone call from the man. He praised me for suggesting he go to see my therapist friend for what had turned out to be some good psychoanalysis. When I asked him if he was out of his depression, he told me, "No!" But he said he was beginning to understand the causes of his depression. He explained that there were a lot of painful things in his past he had psychologically buried, and through the counseling session with my friend he was able to dredge them up and remember them.

He went on to say that what my friend had done for him was very good, but he needed something more. He said when he had been with me, he had sensed that I possessed that special something, and He wanted to see me again. Fortunately, I had a trip to his city scheduled for the following week, and there was time for a get-together. All the doors were open.

When we got together, the man was more than ready to hear what I had to say. Sitting across the table from me in a hotel restaurant, he listened intently as I told him about Jesus and what Jesus had done on the cross. I explained that Jesus not only had taken the punishment for his sins upon Himself, but that Jesus was capable of spiritually invading his heart and mind and *cleansing* him from the sin and guilt that had sapped the joy out of his life. Of all the Bible verses I read to him, none impressed him more than 1 John 1:9:

> If we confess our sins, he is faithful and just to forgive us our
> sins, and to cleanse us from all unrighteousness.

I told him that, in some mystical way, Jesus on the cross could spiritually reach forward in time, invade his mind and heart, and absorb

out of him all the dark things about himself that he had come to recognize and confess as sin during his counseling sessions. As best I could,
I let him know how the Bible declares that Jesus' death for us on the
cross satisfies the heavenly Father's demand that the price for sin be
paid. I explained that *objectively* he need not worry about judgment day
because all the punishment due him had been borne by Jesus on the
cross. I read to him from Isaiah 53:6:

> All we like sheep have gone astray; we have turned every one
> to his own way; and the LORD hath laid on him the iniquity
> of us all.

I then went on to explain that there was also a *subjective* side to
the salvation provided by Christ. I tried to clearly explain that at that
very moment, if he would yield to Christ, Jesus would absorb out of him
all the sin and guilt that was weighing him down emotionally.

In order to explain how all of this works, I resorted to some things
I had learned about Albert Einstein's theory of relativity during my
high-school years. "According to Einstein," I pointed out, "time is relative to motion. What that means is that the faster you travel relative
to the rest of us here on earth, the more time slows down for you.

"If I were to put you in a rocket ship," I told him, "and send you
into space traveling at 160,000 miles per second with instructions to
return in ten years, here's what might happen. Each twenty-four hours
you would mark off a day, and each 365 days you would mark off a year.
And after ten years, you would return. But because, during that ten
years, you had been traveling at 160,000 miles per second relative to us,
when you returned, even though you were only ten years older, you
would find all of us to be twenty years older. Because of the speed you had
been traveling, our twenty years would have been squeezed into ten
years of your time.

"And if it were possible for you to travel 186,000 miles per second
(the speed of light), you would discover that not just our twenty years,
but all of time and history would be squeezed into what could best be
described as *the instantaneous now!*

How God Experiences Time

The reason I went through this simplistic explanation of the relativity theory was to give my friend some idea of how God experiences time. With God, all things happen as they would at the speed of light. The Bible says that with God a thousand years are as a day, and a day as a thousand years (2 Pet. 3:8).

In the Scriptures it says that with God time, as we know it, will be no more. I continued, "Indeed, the very name of God suggests this. His name is Jehovah, or Yahweh, which means, 'I AM THAT I AM.' In a sense, God never was and never shall be. God always IS. Everything is present tense with Him.

"When they asked Jesus who He was, He answered, 'Before Abraham was, I AM!' (John 8:58). He was not using bad grammar here; instead, He was saying something very profound. He was telling us He was God in human form and that what was true of God was true of Him. With Him all things are in the NOW. With Jesus everything is contemporaneous. With God (and that is who Jesus is), every event in human history is simultaneous. He is indeed the Alpha and Omega, the beginning and the end.

"The reason all of this is so important is that Jesus on the cross is not only an objective event that occurred two thousand years ago, but because Jesus *was* and *is* God, the crucifixion is an event that subjectively is happening right here and now. Because Jesus is God, when He hung on the cross two thousand years ago, He could see and experience you sitting across the table from me right now. And at this very instant, if you will let Him, He will absorb into His own body and personality everything about you that is sinful. All your guilt will be drained out of you. Like a sponge, He will absorb it all. Like a magnet, He will at this very moment pull out of you and into Himself all the sin and guilt of your life as though they were iron filings. You can be cleansed and freed from all this spiritual junk that has weighed you down and destroyed your enthusiasm for life."

At that very moment I reached across the table, took my friend's hand, and prayed for that to happen. He repeated after me, "Jesus, You know my sins, and I know my sins. I want to be released from them. Please take them. I beg You."

When we finished the prayer, he was changed. You could see it on his face. He was radiant! He said nothing for about a minute. He just sat there smiling and shaking his head both up and down, and from side to side. And when he did speak, he could only say over and over again, "Oh, thank you! Thank you! Thank you!"

And when I answered, "You're welcome," he said, "Oh, I wasn't talking to you. You can't imagine what I'm feeling right now. There is an incredible lightness to me. I feel like I want to run and jump. There's a happiness I'm feeling that is about to explode. It's going to be hard to restrain me from shouting."

My friend had just had what we call the "born-again" experience. This is the event Jesus referred to when He told Nicodemus:

> "Verily, verily I say unto thee, Except a man be born of water and of the Spirit, he cannot enter into the kingdom of God. That which is born of the flesh is flesh: and that which is born of the Spirit is spirit. Marvel not that I said unto thee, Ye must be born again." (John 3:5–8)

Down through the ages a host of people have had this experience with the same kind of remarkable results.

William James, the famous Harvard psychologist, made a scientific study of such experiences. In his classic book, *The Varieties of Religious Experience*, he wrote:

> To be converted, to be regenerated, to receive grace, to experience religion, to gain assurance, are so many phases which denote the process, gradual or sudden, by which a self hitherto divided, and consciously wrong, inferior and unhappy, becomes unified and consciously right, superior and happy, in consequence of its firmer hold upon religious realities.

Please note that James uses the phrase, "gradual or sudden." For most people it doesn't happen suddenly, as it did with my friend. For most people, becoming a Christian is a growing experience. They let go of their sin little by little, and little by little they grow into the joy of being born again. But what is always the case is that Christian conversion involves surrender. The transition into a new life in Christ occurs when a person consciously acknowledges Jesus Christ as Lord of all of life. It always involves a "letting go." It comes, not because you are willing to do something for Jesus, but because you are willing to let Jesus do something to you. The sin is confessed. The sin that we often love more than we want to admit is finally relinquished to Jesus. And He who never sinned becomes everything about you that is evil:

> For he hath made him to be sin for us, who knew no sin; that
> we might be made the righteousness of God in him. (2 Cor.
> 5:21)

The deliverance from sin that I have been describing can free you for passion. The past need not be a burden that you have to lug around with you. You can be focused with all the spiritual and emotional energy within you on what confronts you in "the now." You can love. You can enter into the beauty of the world around you. You can drink in life and respond with enthusiasm to the Teacher who cries out, *"Carpe Diem!"*

But most important—most significant—and most fulfilling, you can passionately love God. The God whom you once feared because you thought you deserved His condemning judgment will become your friend and the lover of your soul. You will discover the validity of the words of the apostle Paul who wrote, "There is therefore now no condemnation to them which are in Christ Jesus, who walk not after the flesh, but after the Spirit" (Rom. 8:1).

The God who was once far off will then be within you, radiating through your heart and mind and taking the dimness of your soul away (Eph. 2:15–18). Then you will find that there is no joy like the joy of loving God with your whole heart and soul and mind (Matt. 22:37).

Words like *Hallelujah!* and *Praise the Lord!* will come easy. And worship, which once had been a bore, will become a rich time of feeling God flow through you and back to Himself.

17

Making the Best of What Is Yet to Come

*T*he same born-again experience that frees us from the sin and guilt of the past also frees us from the anxieties about the future.

All of us are "creatures oriented unto death," said the great German existentialist philosopher Martin Heidegger. The fear of death is every bit as much the enemy of passionate living as is the curse of sin and guilt. Death has imposed itself on our psyche in subtle but overpowering ways, and unless we overcome the threat that death poses for passionate living, there will be little prospect for joy in our lives and none for loving God. Death is so powerful an enemy that it can take away even our ability to affirm life and worship.

Death's Intrusion on Life

As the consciousness of death overtakes us, we feel a strange and debilitating sickness. Some call it *anxiety*, but that is a word that does

— 127 —

not carry enough emotional punch these days. Consequently, most psychologists and philosophers have adopted another word to carry the meaning of this dark and ominous foreboding, a word that was omnipresent in the writings of the Danish writer and philosopher Soren Kierkegaard and is used with increasing frequency among more recent writers. It is the word *angst*.

Angst was graphically described by a student of mine who was in her late forties when she returned to the university in an attempt to finish her studies. She had just been through a painful divorce and was trying to figure out if there could be any meaning to the rest of her life.

The chairs in the classroom were arranged in a circle, and the twenty or so students who were sitting in them were heavily into a discussion on the Freudian doctrine of *Thanatos* (the Greek word for death). They were reviewing how Freud explained the way in which the fear of death slowly seeps into the consciousness and how we do our best to drive it out. I had just told the class how the attempt to repress the consciousness of our mortality is, according to Freud, the basis of all of our phobias. I had explained that vertigo comes from the fear of falling into the abyss of nothingness at the end of life, that agoraphobia comes from the fear of being buried, and that claustrophobia is the fear that arises from the threat of being enclosed in a casket and dropped into a grave.

I asked my students if they understood what Freud was saying about how the fear of death affects us. And when the students assured me they did grasp what I had been teaching them, this woman spoke up.

There was sarcasm in her voice and condescension in her demeanor. She was scornful of the students' assertion that they understood the threat of death as I had laid it out in the classroom discussion. "You don't know what death is and what it does to people while they are alive. The phobias described by Freud don't even get near what's involved," she said.

I will never forget the frozen, silent shock that fell over the class following her sudden outburst. She had seemed like a harmless middle-aged woman up until then. None of us could have anticipated this sudden and almost vicious attack on us. She expressed a disgusted impatience with her younger classmates who had listened to my lecture, jotted down a few notes, and then thought they understood what it means to feel life being drained of its vitality as it moves inexorably toward death. And then again, there was a sense that her anger might not so much be directed toward the students as toward herself and what was happening to her. The awareness of her impending mortality increasingly infringed upon what was left of her life, especially after being "thrown away" for a younger woman.

"It's different than you think. I do not suffer from any of those Freudian phobias that you are describing," she said to me. "I suffer in different ways." Then, directing herself toward the students, she slowly and deliberately tried to explain.

"Imagine yourself at an organ recital. You are enjoying the music when you think you detect something that has gone wrong. It sounds as though a key on the organ is stuck. You think you hear a dissonant note. I say *think* because at first you aren't sure. You are only aware of it during the pauses in the music. But as the recital continues, the disturbing sound from the stuck key gets louder and louder until it cannot be ignored. Even when other notes are sounded and huge chords are struck, it is there. It intrudes on everything you hear. And still it gets louder and louder until, try as you may, it makes listening to what is left of the music unbearable. Death has intruded on my life like that. It has robbed me in ways you will understand only when you are where I am."

Suddenly there was a painful sadness in the air. Any flippancy about what had been an academic matter just a few minutes earlier was gone. The heaviness of the moment made going on impossible, and I could only dismiss class without comment.

When we met the next day, the class went on without any allusion to the awesome confession of the day before. We all seemed to pretend it hadn't happened. It wasn't that we thought that discussion might embarrass the woman who had disrupted the class. She wasn't there to be embarrassed. None of us ever saw her again; she never returned to class.

Perhaps, having revealed herself, she feared what we might do with what she had told us. As for the rest of us, we simply, but awkwardly, went on to other things. Avoidance, you see, is not only a defense mechanism for individuals. Groups sometimes practice it too. It's a survival technique.

If Soren Kierkegaard had been that woman's teacher, he might have been able to handle things better. The man whom historians refer to as "that disturbing Dane" might have empathized with her in a healing manner. Kierkegaard once wrote, "Life is a novel, about a man who goes insane, and the author finishes writing in the first person." He would have been well aware of the kind of *angst* my former student was suffering. Kierkegaard, who once said, "As our lives unfold, at first we yawn, but later the yawn turns into a scream," might have known what to say.

But perhaps Kierkegaard's most telling statement concerning *angst* was this: "We are all like smooth pebbles thrown so as to skim and dance over the surface of water. But we feel ourselves running out of momentum, and we fear that the inevitable moment is coming when there will be nothing left but to sink into a hundred thousand fathoms of nothingness." I think that was how my angry student felt.

As with sin and guilt, even those who deny that they are anxious about death are deeply troubled by it. Subconsciously, *angst* eats away at our vitality and joy. Life loses its childlike spontaneity and excitement. Little by little everything becomes jaded. As Kierkegaard once said, "There comes a time when not even Beethoven is enough." We are usually perplexed by this loss of *joie de vivre* because we are unaware of what is robbing us of it. We are afraid to name the cause because we know that once we do, it will become even more real. Some of us put on a false bravado as we lift our glasses and try boldly to declare the Epicurean dictum, "Eat, drink, and be merry, for tomorrow we die." But alas, we don't. And on the morrow the emptiness of that cry gives us a more painful pause, for we are more aware than ever that we must live with death without the deliverance that death itself can bring. "Denial," says one of my friends, "is not just a river in Egypt." And all of our efforts to deny death its due are doomed to futility.

An Antidote for the Sin-Sick Soul

Once again, Jesus comes with the antidote. The poison of the consciousness of death can be countered. There really is a balm in Gilead that heals the sin-sick soul (Jer. 8:22). It comes in the resurrection of Christ. In telling the salvation story, we should not only announce that we are delivered from the psychic dissipation caused by sin and guilt, but we should also declare that through the resurrection of Christ, death has lost its power over us.

My father-in-law, Robert Davidson, was one of the more saintly men I have known. He was the faithful pastor of four Baptist churches and gained the allegiance of each congregation because he truly cared for them. He loved his Jesus, and he loved the people Jesus had given him to serve. He loved the Bible, and he loved to pray.

In his later years, Dad gradually lost touch with reality. Or at least he lost touch with the reality that the rest of us live in. He became detached and reticent. But even in his disengagement from the people around him, he showed us a Christ-like character. The hardening of his arteries and all the loss of memory that that malady can bring could not take away his almost ethereal smile that seemed to say, in the words of his favorite hymn, "It is well with my soul."

More and more Dad slipped away from us, and at family gatherings he would simply sit silently at the dinner table, apparently unable to participate or take in the talk of the family. But still he would wear the smile that to me gave evidence of his peace with God.

One Saturday my wife came home from visiting her parents, visibly upset. She wondered how much longer her mother would be able to care for her dad at home. His mind and body were failing fast. Peggy was still troubled as she went to bed that night.

Very early the next morning, Peggy received a call from her mother with the good news that Dad would not be going into any kind of healthcare facility because he had gone Home to his heavenly Father. Peggy's peace was complete when her mother related the circumstances of Dad's death.

They, too, had had a troubled night, she said. Dad was unable to get comfortable and had not slept at all. Mother had prayed, "If only he could get a few hours' sleep."

Then, at about 4:30 on Sunday morning, Dad suddenly began to recite in a strong voice these verses of Scripture from 1 Corinthians:

> O death, where is thy sting? O grave, where is thy victory?
> The sting of death is sin; and the strength of sin is the law.
> But thanks be to God, which giveth us the victory through
> our Lord Jesus Christ. (1 Cor. 15:55–57)

My mother-in-law is not sure whether Dad was preaching, comforting her, or reassuring himself, but she *is* sure he knew he was dying, and he was ready to go. He recited the passage three times in all, each time with greater assurance than before. Then, within the hour, he slipped peacefully away to his heavenly Father.

Dad's dying, like his living, was ample evidence that death need not have debilitating power over us. In his dying hour, my father-in-law gave testimony that death does not have to be the final word about life.

Those who reflect on death tell us the threat of hell is not the cause of our fears. Rejecting a belief in an afterlife where our sins will find us out will not deliver us from the frightening consequences of being creatures aware of their dying. As a matter of fact, abolishing hell from our consciousness only makes matters worse. Hell, we discover upon analysis, is by no means as threatening as the fears generated by nihilism. The threat of non-being, contend the existentialists, philosophers, and psychologists, is a far greater threat than any that can be posed by the fear of the fiery furnace.

The Gospel's Declaration against a Dismal Message

Perhaps one of the greatest ironies of modernity is that we have a sophisticated intelligentsia that has done away with a literal hell *after* death only to create a psychological hell *before* death with their threat of non-being after death. There is no comfort in nihilism. Those who tell us that life is all there is offer us no comfort. I find that none of those nihilistic existentialists who preached a call to be courageous and to create meaning out of the absurdity of our lives were examples of people who lived lives of joyful celebration. All of them were morbid people who, for the most part, lived lives that were as tragic as the death they believed brought life to an end.

Over and against the dismal message of the worldly philosophers stands the declaration of the gospel. Because Christ Jesus lives, we Christians assert with confidence that we also shall live (1 Cor. 15:12–25). We have hope in Him. We are convinced that the same Spirit who invaded His body and brought Him back to life will resuscitate our mortal bodies. This is at the core of our faith, and it is the basis of our rescuing hope. We accept the good news:

> But if the Spirit of him that raised up Jesus from the dead dwell in you, he that raised up Christ from the dead shall also quicken your mortal bodies by his Spirit that dwelleth in you. (Rom. 8:11)

It is this truth that drives out the *angst* and frees us to be passionately involved in life in the here and now. It is this assurance of eternal life and this hope of glory that enables us to love God with heart and soul and mind.

The deliverance out of *angst* into joy was presented to me in dramatic contrast when I was asked to participate in a seminar on death and dying. The meeting was held at the College of Physicians in Philadelphia, and it drew several hundred doctors, psychotherapists, and gerontologists.

What proved to me to be the most interesting event of the day was a panel discussion on attitudes toward death among those who were residents of religiously sponsored institutions for the elderly. On the panel were a Roman Catholic priest, an evangelical minister, and an Orthodox Jewish rabbi. Each of them was a chaplain, and each of them spent most of his time getting people ready to die.

There were many dramatic contrasts between what the different chaplains reported about their experiences, but none were so great as the contrasts between the words of the rabbi and the words of the minister. The rabbi pointed out that in Orthodox Jewish tradition there is no clear-cut doctrine promising life after death. "There are some hopes and some maybes. But there is nothing specific," he reported. "It wasn't until what you Christians call the Inter-Testament Period that a belief in the afterlife appeared in Judaism. If you go by just the Scriptures we Orthodox Jews believe to be given by God, you have nothing on this subject."

The rabbi went on to explain that the elderly people he served had very little in the way of a belief that there was anything after this life ends. Then, with candid honesty, he went on to describe how an immobilizing depression grew in his people as the specter of dying came closer with every passing day. "In some cases," he told us, "there is even terror and overpowering despair."

"Most of my people," he reported, "die little by little for a long time before they die."

In contrast to this morbid description by the Orthodox rabbi was the response of the evangelical minister. He almost seemed embarrassed to speak after the depressing descriptions of dying he had just heard. There was a somewhat apologetic tone to his voice as he told the group that most of his people faced death with a fair amount of optimism, and that for those whose personal faith and belief systems were strong there was even a pronounced sense of growing joy.

This minister told one particular story that touched all of us. It was about a ninety-five-year-old woman who would always greet him with the words, "Well, Pastor, it won't be long. It won't be long. Any day now I'll be seeing Him face to face. It might be today. But even if it's not, it won't be long." The possibility of death, rather than creating angst, actually was a source of joyful expectation. She was able to affirm life with enthusiasm because death no longer encroached on it as an enemy. Instead of being afraid of the future, the future for her invaded the present with hope and made the present a good place to be.

Embracing Life with Passion and Love

To be able to love God passionately requires an assurance of our deliverance from sin and death. The psalmist let it be known that there was no way He could call out to God or express his love for God if death and the threat of death overpowered him (Psalm 22).

The promise of eternal life is not just to free us from angst. It is also meant to free us to love God, and, as the Westminster Catechism says, enjoy Him forever. In an ultimate sense, to embrace life with a passion and to love God with the fullness of our humanity are one and the same thing. We cannot do one without the other. God sent His Son to provide us with life and to give it to us more abundantly. And that abundant life expresses itself in loving God. There should be a passion in the way we express ourselves in worship. It was in order for us to feel this passion that He freed us from anything that would stifle it.

PART VII

COMING ALIVE TO NATURE

18

Going to the Garden Alone

*O*nce I had a chance to get to know a Franciscan monk. We were together at an ecumenical conference held at some out-of-the-way retreat center in the Upper Peninsula of Michigan. I was to be the main speaker for the conference, and this Franciscan brother was supposed to lead the group in meditation and worship.

Being from an activistic Baptist background, the whole style of my brown-robed brother seemed strange to me, and certainly the times of meditation he directed were foreign to my kind of religion. I was out to save the world, and I was impatient with contemplation and reflection. It was not that I was against what he was into, it was just that I could not see any practical results coming from it. To my way of thinking, the cloistered life was an escape from the real world and a disengagement from the responsibility to deal with the problems that plague society.

By the second day of the conference, I was getting tired of the spiritual trip this Franciscan monk was directing us to take. I was fidgeting during the times of meditation, and I was receiving no revelations from what seemed like endless periods of reflection. I did my best to feel God speaking to me in the midst of quietude, but nothing happened. It took until the end of the second day for me to get the courage to ask the monk what I was supposed to get out of the spiritual routines he was prescribing, and why I was failing at them. I had done everything I had been told. The previous night I had sat alone under the stars as I had been instructed and thought how beautiful they were. But that was not what I thought being spiritual was all about. And as I meditated by the stream, I felt good, but nothing more. Whatever blessings I received from God were blessings I could have received anywhere and anytime as long as my heart was right.

The answer I got was that I did not know how to experience nature as a sacrament.

Like Electricity through a Wire

Being Baptist, the very word *sacrament* was outside my understanding of spirituality. For Baptists the Lord's Supper and baptism are what we call *ordinances*. They are "object lessons" and reminders of the fact that Jesus allowed His body to be nailed to the cross and was willing to shed His blood in a substitutionary atonement. Baptism, for me, was a kind of living sermon "preached" to let observers know that in Christ my old life was dead and buried, and I had been raised up to a new life as a follower of Christ. The former was symbolized when I went down into the water, and the latter was symbolized when the minister pulled me out of the water and stood me up. These ordinances were important messages, but nothing more. They had only as much meaning as I put into them, I believed, and nothing more. And now this monk was trying to tell this Baptist, who didn't even believe in the sacraments, that I was supposed to treat nature sacramentally.

"God is not nature, and nature is not God," he declared. "To think that would be to think like a pantheist and not a Christian. But God is *in* nature; He permeates nature. He comes through it like electricity comes through a wire. The wire is not the electricity, but it can be a vehicle through which the electricity flows. God is not the stars and the moon, but He is in every molecule of the stars and the moon. He is a presence in every atom, holding the electron and protons and neutrons together. Without Him all things would fly apart. By His presence all things consist. And by His grace you can feel His presence in these creations of God. The God who transcends the creation uses His creation sacramentally to bless us and, when we feel Him coming into us through His creation, we enjoy Him in ways that are unique and are a special means of His grace.

"The next time you sit under the stars or sit by a babbling brook, listen to God. Ask Him to speak to you through His creation and to awaken you to His presence in the miracle of His physical world. Ask Him to open your eyes to see and your ears to hear. He promises to answer, and you will hear Him speak. Be patient and wait patiently on the Lord, and you will hear Him over the sound of the wind and from beyond the sound of the running, splashing water. You will even hear Him in the pinpoints of light that decorate the darkness of the night. He gives ears to hear what has no sound and eyes to see what is invisible. Empty yourself, and He will flow into you if you invite Him.

"Surrender to Him, and He will feed you with His glory. You try too hard," he said. "You cannot go to Him. You can only yield to His coming to you through the majesty of His creation."

And then he said this: "Look closely at something long enough, and you will find that it begins to look back at you."

That was the most intriguing thing he said.

Enraptured by a World Totally New

The next night I went to the garden alone. I sat myself down on the side of the hill by the edge of the stream. There was no moon. Only the morning star and a myriad countless other stars were over my head. And I waited. I prayed for nothing but God. I wanted to taste Him and smell Him and feel Him and enjoy Him. And I waited and waited and waited.

I have no idea how long it was before I fell into a deep sleep. Nor do I have any idea how long I slept. What I do know is that when I awoke, everything around me was ablaze with God. As I opened my eyes, I found I had been transported into another world. There were stars and hills and a babbling brook in this new world, and although they resembled the stars and hills and brook in the world I had left behind, they were totally new. Life was coming at me from all of these inanimate creations. I felt myself being bombarded by the Holy Spirit. Holiness was coming from under and over and around everything. Even the ground on which I sat was holy, and the glory of the Lord was burning in the bushes around me. The things that were in the world were not of it. Everything was changed, and yet nothing had changed. It was I who had changed. Before I even realized what I was doing, I was on my feet and running. Never did my feet move faster or my body feel lighter. Never before did I run with such abandon. Up the side of the hill I ran, faster and faster, as I reached for the top. Stronger and stronger I grew as my arms pumped with joy. It was only my lungs that hurt. The air seemed thin, and I grew short of breath. When I reached the summit, I threw myself to the ground and stretched spread-eagle before my God. I could hear the pounding of my heart and the rush of blood to my head, and I thought I would die and I did not care. I was already raptured, and I was already tasting the world that is to come. As it was for some men of old, I was on the top of the mountain, and I would have stayed there forever. But I didn't.

What I share with you about the relationship of spiritual conversion to a new awareness of nature is not unique or original. It is not in any way rare. If you take the time to study the accounts of those who have yielded to the grace of God and who have been open to what the Holy Spirit wants to do in them, you will find that they all hold such a changed perspective on the world in common.

William James, the brilliant Harvard psychologist and philosopher, made a survey of those kinds of religious experiences; he reported on them in his classic Gifford lectures at Edinburgh. Over and over again he found in the biographies of those he called "the converted" the same kind of experiences. As an example, James cited what the staid Puritan Jonathan Edwards had to say upon his conversion:

"The appearance of everything was altered; there seemed to be, as it were, a calm, sweet cast, or appearance of divine glory, in almost everything. God's excellency, his wisdom, his purity and love, seemed to appear in everything; in sun, moon and stars; in the clouds and blue sky; in the grass, flowers and trees; in the water and all nature; which used greatly to fix my mind. And scarce anything, among all the works of nature, was so sweet to me as thunder and lightning; formerly nothing had been so terrible to me. Before, I used to be uncommonly terrified with thunder, and to be struck with terror when I saw a thunderstorm rising; but now, on the contrary, it rejoices me."

Another of James's many examples is from the conversion of the illiterate English evangelist Billy Bray, who said:

"I praised God with my whole heart . . . I remember this, that everything looked new to me, the people, the fields, the cattle, the trees. I was like a new man in a new world. . . . I can't help praising the Lord. As I go along the street, I lift up one foot, and it seems to say, 'Glory'; and I lift up the other, and it seems to say, 'Amen'; and so they keep up like that all the time I am walking."

James also studied stories of the not-so-famous Christians who entered into this kind of spirituality. He quoted one man, a simple farmer, who gave just as eloquent a report when telling what followed his conversion:

"When I went in the morning into the fields to work, the glory of God appeared in all His visible creation. I well remembered we reaped oats, and how every straw and head of the oats seemed, as it were, arrayed in a kind of rainbow glory, or to glow, if I may so express it, in the glory of God."

Such things do not happen to everyone. And when these moments of spiritual aliveness do come, they are only for a while.

The ecstasy does not last forever. All who experience it must come down from the mountain. There is always the mundane on the other side of the silence that speaks. But for those who have been invaded by the presence and have tasted the boundless joy, there is an aliveness that pervades the body and a heightened awareness of how precious all of life really is. You notice things. You enjoy things. You are entertained by simple things. Old things have passed away, and everything has become new.

Herbert Marcuse, in his book *One Dimensional Man*, makes it clear that he understood all too well what I have been describing. Not that he ever claimed such an experience for himself. His atheism did not lend his consciousness too readily to the mystical. But he recognized that for many people the physical world is not one-dimensional. There are people who experience something more than the empirical when they encounter the physical world; they know there is something more than what is physically *there*. Marcuse, a sociologist who made his reputation by analyzing and explaining revolutions, recognized that such mystical consciousness provides one of the most powerful creators of revolutionary movements. Once one has experienced the transcendent, he said, one can never again be content with the world that is. There is a discontentment with the mundane world that makes it difficult for totalitarian rulers to convince their subjects that they ought to be satisfied with what is provided by the dominant political-economic system.

A New and Passionate Eroticism

Those who have tasted transcendental reality can never again be convinced that this world and the society that regulates them can satisfy their needs. Those who have tasted of the heavenly gift will always hunger because they know there is more to life, and that something more is not controlled by the system but lies beyond anything that the rulers of the system can provide. Out of such holy discontentment new movements are born. The sense of what is absent makes us discontented with what is present.

The most interesting thing that happened to me on that hillside in Michigan was that I became a lover of nature. I loved it, not because of what it was and is, but for what came through it and what it could become to anyone who surrenders to its wonder. A new and passionate eroticism entered my relationship with nature. A kind of *libido* was released that night. My love affair with nature was more than just a mental or psychological thing. There was a pleasurable feeling in my bones and a sense of release of tension in my muscles. They were sensations I thought belonged only to the realm of the sexual.

When I told my Franciscan friend about these unexpected effects of my encounter with the sacred, he smiled and said, "Now do you understand why we celibate monks are satiated? Do you get some sense as to where we find contentment that some think can never be known save in the arms of a woman?"

Again, I say, Marcuse would have understood. In his analysis of our modern one-dimensional society, he made the point that, in earlier times, when alienation from nature was not so severe, eroticism was more diffused. Marcuse explained that there were people in another time who experienced passionate love with all the world. These were the people who sensed the mysterious *tremendom* in all they saw and touched and smelled and heard. Such saints were erotically stimulated by everything. Nothing for them was prosaic. Everything was poetic. The life-giving energy of eros seemed to flow out of everything around them, and Thanatos, the death force, seemed to have lost its sting. Death was overcome in victory, and its power was unable to threaten either young or old.

Marcuse explained that as humanity entered the era of modernity and all but the rational categories were excluded from experience people still had the hunger for erotic satiation. But the rationalists taught us that the only eroticism was sexual and that it was only through the sexual that we would find the release that would leave us with a sense of fulfillment and well-being. And that is why we have become a people preoccupied with sex. We expect all of our erotic appetites to be gratified through orgasms.

Not being satisfied, we go out and buy books to tell us how to make it last longer, be more intense and even provide multiple orgasms. When what was supposed to be received by many means is reduced to being experienced by only one means, then that one means becomes too important. When the joy of the erotic gets narrowed down to an occasional physical convulsion, than that convulsion takes on too much significance and comes to be viewed as the purpose for living. God never meant for it to be like this.

19

Hugging a Tree Isn't As Ridiculous As It Sounds

*D*o not suppose that those to whom we usually refer as religious people are delivered from the inability to experience erotic ecstasy from nature. Sadly, there is an antimystical quality to much of what goes on in our churches. Worship, particularly in Protestant churches, tends to be so rationalistic that seldom is there any hint that life ought to be riddled through with the quality of the miraculous. Sermons are, for the most part, lectures designed to reduce what is incomprehensible to reasonable explanations. But faith is not so much a set of rational propositions as it is an intensive trust growing out of a passionate love for God. Many solid church members can readily give a *reason* for the faith that lies within them but seem almost devoid of having really *felt* God. Most Methodists I know have never even come near to having their hearts "strangely warmed" in an ecstatic surrender to the Holy Spirit as did their founder, John Wesley. It's a long way from Aldersgate Street, where Wesley had the spiritual awakening that made him a passionate lover of God and of people, to where they live today.

There are few Catholics who have tasted what Francis did on the mountain or what Blaise Pascal tasted when he was caught up in the fire and joy of the Lord as he sat alone one night in his bedroom. No wonder most Christians do not get from nature what these mystics of the past could. Religion has become propositional truth rather than passionate love. It is rationality rather than ecstasy. It is thought in the mind, but not felt in the heart. It prepares people for heaven instead of making them passionately alive on earth.

Claiming the Gift of Life

It doesn't have to be this way. You can make yourself ready to receive the gift of life if you want it. The enlivening power that comes from being filled with the Holy Spirit cannot be controlled and made into a "thing" that can be delivered on demand to anyone who has the right formula or knows how to push the right biblically prescribed buttons. The Spirit bloweth where it wills. You cannot tell when it will come or how (John 3:8). It is a gift poured out by the grace of God. However, there is much you can do to prepare yourself to receive this blessing. There are steps you can take so that when the Spirit does come you will not be passed by.

First there is repentance. It is a good thing to go to a quiet place. It may be on a hillside or in a closet. There ought to be a secret place where you can go away and be with God. Even if you do not sense His presence, He is there because He is God and God is always there. Then you must grow still and consider what it is about you that would be offensive to God. Name those things that you are and do that are unclean. Once they are named, they lose their power. Once they are confessed, they can be cleansed.

> If we confess our sins, he is faithful and just to forgive us our
> sins, and to cleanse us from all unrighteousness. (1 John 1:9)

God, in His love, is faithful. That means He will not fail you. Do not simply run through a list of the sins and ugliness in your life. Take time to hate them one by one. You will never be free of them if you pray as Augustine once prayed:

> Oh, Lord! Deliver me from lust!
> But not yet.

Hate your sin with what the Bible calls a perfect hatred. Hate it so much that you passionately want it purged. With the psalmist cry out:

> Purge me with hyssop, and I shall be clean: wash me, and I shall be whiter than snow. Make me to hear joy and gladness; that the bones which thou has broken may rejoice. Hide thy face from my sins, and blot out all mine iniquities. Create in me a clean heart, O God; and renew a right spirit within me. (Ps. 51:7–10)

Second, focus on Jesus. This is hard because the mind tends to bounce around like a ping-pong ball. It is not easy to keep the mind fixed on God, but the Scripture says, "Thou wilt keep him in perfect peace, whose mind is stayed on thee" (Isa. 26:3). I find it useful sometimes just to think of words that express some of the things that are true about Him. I simply pray, "Lord, You are so loving, so kind, so tender, so good, so forgiving, such a friend"—and the list goes on. I not only say each word, but I meditate on how I have experienced each of those things I say about Him. I think of ways I have recently seen the effects of His love or how His tender mercies have been extended to me. In this extended time I become focused on Him; I think of nothing else. I do not ask for anything. I do not make any pleas on behalf of friends or family, regardless of how much they may be in need of His caring attention. I just think about how good and wonderful He is and thank Him continuously for being who He is.

If You Look Long Enough . . .

Being focused on Jesus changes me. It clears away those thoughts that would cloud Him out. It raises me to a new level of consciousness.

It makes me ready to receive Him. Then it is time to let the Jesus you adore come at you and into you. When you have emptied yourself of all but Christ you become aware of Him in what was, just a short time ago, only the natural world. The world becomes holy. The world becomes glorified by Him, and the natural becomes the vehicle for the supernatural. Or, to use the word of my Franciscan friend, *sacramental*. Then you can embrace the world with passion and, like Saint Francis, call the sun, moon, and stars your brothers and sisters. Because the ultimate Brother and Sister is flowing through them. And there can be communion with nature because you can sense that the same Lord who is in you is the Lord of Creation and is manifesting His mysterious self through His creation (Col. 1:15–18).

If it does not happen at once, remember that the apostles waited for forty days before the Spirit fell upon them (Acts 2:1–4). Hang in there. "In due season we shall reap, if we faint not" (Gal. 6:9). The passionate aliveness to the glories of nature that comes with the gift will make the waiting unworthy to be compared with the price.

Remember, if you look closely at something long enough, it will begin to look back at you.

There is a postscript and warning to this discussion about a passionate involvement with nature. The warning is simply this: To love nature is to want to care for it and work to save it from destructive exploitation and the ugly scars of careless use. In all likelihood you will become one of those "tree-huggers." You will end up trying to save the whales, rescue the rain forests and getting into some of the other things that conservationists place high on their agenda. You will become environmentally concerned. If that scares you or seems to be a cause in which only strange people get involved, then I have some good news for you.

Doing Your Part to Rescue Creation

There are Christians who are really trying to be friends with environmentalists. It would seem that this should be a natural friendship. Those who love the Creator ought to find it easy to relate to those who love His creation. But such has not been the case.

Christians, particularly evangelicals, have tended to ally with those conservative capitalists who fear that the consequences of environmentalism will be detrimental to the American economy. They worry that environmentalists will make concern for spotted owls more important than jobs for loggers and that clean-air regulations will make American industry noncompetitive. An even greater fear among evangelical Christians has been generated by the discovery that the New Age Movement has made environmentalism one of its primary causes. Christians find it impossible to participate in the activities of Earth Day without rubbing shoulders with people who are into crystals or some other occult activities as part of nature worship, and they are quite intimidated by all of this.

From the other side, environmentalists also have a lot of fear and suspicion about Christians. They often accuse us of propagating a theology that leads to the destructive exploitation of nature. They have been duped into believing that Christians make the biblical mandate to subdue the earth (Gen. 1:28) into an ideology that justifies all kind of abuses, from the decimation of rain forests to the hunting of endangered species into extinction.

These respectively distorted perceptions have created a great deal of totally unnecessary misunderstanding and hostility. However, there is now a group that is trying to remedy the problem and to be reconcilers between these sometimes warring groups. It is the Christian Environmental Association (CEA) based in Fremont, California. Those who make up this group are, at the same time, deeply in love with Christ and deeply concerned with ecological issues.

As evangelicals, the members of CEA are committed to sharing their faith in Christ with those who are in environmental movements. They plan to show up at Earth Day celebrations all across America with the specific purpose of drawing environmentalists into a personal relationship with Jesus. CEA is convinced that the Green Movement, as environmentalists refer to themselves, cannot realize its full potential for rescuing nature without coming under the Lordship of Christ. CEA members are calling on fellow Christians to join them in their efforts.

CEA members argue that Christians have been called by God to be in the world like leaven. They believe that Christians should be in the Green Movement as a transforming presence helping this movement to be all that Jesus would want it to be. They say that if Christians are to be the salt of the earth they cannot retreat from reasonable and concerned environmental movements.

"Join us!" CEA begs church people. "Help us evangelize our Green Movement brothers and sisters so that together we can rescue nature in a God-honoring way."

The Christian Environmental Association has a plan that should intrigue environmentalists. CEA plans to buy up the rain forests. As wild and outrageous as that may seem, if you stop to think about it, it is the only way the rain forests really can be saved. The companies that now own much of this incredible natural resource are not about to leave it undeveloped simply because some concerned "Greenies" mount a massive letter-writing campaign against them. And the poor countries of Latin America and Africa where most of the rain forests can be found are not about to let them just sit there. These poor countries have to sell off the rain forests regardless of long-range consequences simply to be able to handle their present debts and have the resources to meet current desperate needs.

If Christians don't like what those who have been buying the rain forests are doing with them, then they, themselves, should become the buyers, contend the members of the Christian Environmental Association. And they invite people of goodwill both inside and outside the church to join them in this effort.

CEA people are not unrealistic dreamers. They have already bought two thousand acres of rain forest in Belize, a tropical country in Central America. They have started a campaign to get churches, youth groups, Sunday school classes, and a host of concerned individual Christians to join in. It only costs one hundred dollars to buy an acre. Instead of complaining about what is happening to the environment, you or your church group can buy some land and be partners in this bold venture. Furthermore, CEA invites secular groups from Girl Scout troops to Rotary clubs to join them and to help to purchase this precious environmental resource.

Roy Goble, a businessman and the founder of CEA, has come up with a brilliantly creative way to get some of the money needed to buy some of this land: Recycling cans! When crushed and sold to a recycling agency every aluminum can yields, by Goble's calculations, enough money to buy eight square feet of rain forest. Think of it! A church youth group could buy up and save a big chunk of rain forest simply by staging a recycling campaign.

At last Christian people have a chance to live out their discipleship toward the environment in a balanced manner. They can join CEA and share in making the gospel relevant to a lot of hitherto uninterested "Green people" and, at the same time, be part of a concrete effort that will make a difference when it comes to saving the earth without worshiping nature.

Just write to:

Christian Environmental Association
48835 Kato Road
P.O. Box 15026
Fremont, California 94539-2026

You might even want to send along a check for a hundred dollars and buy an acre of the jungles of Belize.

PART VIII

COMING ALIVE
IN MARRIAGE

20

Where Have All the Flowers Gone?

*M*arriage without passion is marriage that many people find intolerable. It can even be said that the reason divorce has become so common is because people will no longer put up with marriages that are simply comfortable arrangements. "If there is no passion in their marriage, they want out."

Some have called it the "Peggy Lee Syndrome," after the singer whose hit song was a reflection on love and marriage, asking the simple question, "Is that all there is?"

But regardless of what we call it, there is a sense of disappointment among many married people, and that disappointment is related to the failure of the marital relationship to deliver the passion expected of it. Sex manuals promising that new techniques for making love will re-kindle passion and bring new life to marriage deliver little. Disappointment usually turns to cynicism. Some find help in counseling. But in many cases even that fails.

There are those who try extramarital affairs on the side with the hope that newness and intrigue will provide deliverance from the deadness of their marriages. It is far too simple to think of them as immoral when they are driven not so much by lust as by a desperate urge to experience something that gives life.

To make matters worse, most people have been led to believe if they can just find that "one great love," their every need and emotional hunger will be gratified. "If there is no passion in the activities of everyday life, it doesn't matter," they say to themselves, because they believe that someday and somewhere there is that one great love that will dispel all emptiness and end all dryness of the soul. That was the lesson they learned from the romantics, whose novels and movies served as instruments of hope in their arid lives.

We should be careful not to look upon those who buy into this myth as an inferior group of tickytack conformists whom we more enlightened critics transcend. Most of us have believed the myth for at least part of our lives, and many of us believe in it still. We are partially products of our culture and, disappointments not withstanding, it is all too common to harbor some of the hopes our culture carries. Even those of us who ought to know better often harbor the belief that deliverance from deadness into all-fulfilling passion can be ours if we can just share love with the right person.

Sociological studies indicate that the romantic feelings that accompany the honeymoon diminish more than 80 percent in intensity during the first two years of marriage. With the decline of romance the excitement gets lost, and the passion usually fades away.

Go into a restaurant and look around. You don't have to be a trained social scientist to figure out what you see. As your eyes move from table to table, you may spot a couple who are in the throes of "first love." They seem engrossed with each other. They hang on each other's every word. Their faces are animated. Every moment seems precious to them, and as they laugh at one another's jokes and seem to be agreeing with every profound insight being shared, you might even wonder if their excitement with each other will ever end.

You don't have to go far for the answer to that one. A further glance around the restaurant will no doubt bring you to another couple who will provide a sad contrast. You just know this second couple has been married a while and they have settled in for an arrangement that is just that—an arrangement.

He looks angry, and she looks sad. He seems to be staring at the floor, and her eyes seem wistfully unfocused as though aimed at nothing. They have already given their orders to the waitress and have nothing to say to each other as they wait for the food to be delivered.

It is hard to even imagine that this husband and wife were once animated lovers who could lose themselves in each other's eyes, and who believed that having found each other was the wildest miracle in time and history. But such was probably true. Now it is hard to believe that once upon a time their greatest hunger was just to be together. It is painful to watch them just sit there passively while they wait for their burgers and fries.

This doesn't have to happen. Relationships that once burned with passion need not dissipate into dead indifference. The fading of emotion in personal relationships is not an inevitability. The gospel declares otherwise. If a marriage seems dead, remember that every Easter is an evidence of resurrection, and every Christmas tells us there can be a rebirth of love. But it takes discipline and effort to make a marriage live. And finding out just what needs to be done to make and keep marriage passionate must become our focus.

The Renewal of Passion

The renewal of passion starts with a decision. It is a decision to care. It begins when a sacred discontentment with deadness rises to the level of consciousness and the individual says, "No! I'm not going to settle for this! I'm not going to go on like this! I know there can be more, and I'm going after it."

A forty-year-old woman lets it be known that she's just waiting for the last child to leave home, then she is going to leave too. "I want more out of life than this marriage will let me have," she quietly moans.

And then there's the forty-five-year-old man who is drowning in a marital relationship that has smothered his zest for life. He declares, "It's time to come up for air."

In no way do I approve of what these emotionally hungry people are about to do, but I find something hopeful in the fact that each of them has at least awakened to the reality that his or her marriage is little more than a catatonic condition. At least people like this have stepped out from the crowd that goes to sleep somewhere in their midtwenties and never wakes up again.

It is hard to pinpoint what causes a person to face up to the reality that a marriage has gone dead. Sometimes art can make it happen. Profound things are felt sometimes in a poem or a piece of music. Really good art does not so much reveal what is there (unartistic photos can do that) as it reminds us of what is not there. It stirs an uneasy awareness about life and, like a cock crowing, reminds us that we have betrayed what we promised to keep alive " 'til death do us part."

Sometimes what sets us off is horrendous news. A woman is diagnosed as having breast cancer, and because she realizes that the quantity of her days is now frighteningly limited, the quality of these days becomes urgently important.

One of the best "wake-up calls" to life and love comes simply by reading the Scriptures. The psalmist puts it into words for us:

> LORD, make me to know mine end, and the measure of my days, what it is; that I may know how frail I am. Behold, thou hast made my days as an handbreadth; and mine age is as nothing before thee: verily every man at his best state is altogether vanity. Selah. Surely every man walketh in a vain shew: surely they are disquieted in vain: he heapeth up riches, and knoweth not who shall gather them. (Ps. 39:4–6)

And the cynic of the book of Ecclesiastes describes it too:

> Vanity of vanities, saith the Preacher, vanity of vanities; all is vanity. What profit hath a man of all his labour which he taketh under the sun? (Eccles. 1:2–3)

But we don't have to read these "down" passages to be led to reflect on the deadness that has come to pervade our lives. The contrast that we experience when we read about those who seem fully alive in the Spirit can shake us up. To read about Jacob's love for Rachel in the Old Testament and to feel what love can be as we read 1 Corinthians 13 will do it.

"I want to be married to somebody like Jesus," a woman said to me as she and her husband sat in my office for marriage counseling. "I don't mean somebody who's perfect or has the power to be a messiah. I mean somebody who knows how to feel things like Jesus did. I wish I were married to somebody who could feel my hurts and know what rages in my soul without having to be told."

"So do I," her husband said quietly. "So do I."

But this couple was better off than most. They knew how sick they were. And Jesus said that only those who know they are sick are likely to go to the Great Physician. Only those who sense a silent emptiness of life in general and about marriage in particular are likely to make the decisions that can lead to deliverance. Regrettably, most of those who realize they have lost their first love and decide they have to do something about it end up doing the wrong thing. They get divorced. They do not recognize that in the overwhelming number of cases, their marriages could be salvaged and made into exciting and enlivening relationships. They think new partners will bring them what they are looking for, when in reality the best possibilities for passion in marriage can be found in working things out right where they are. New marriages are not the answer. What most people need is a new approach to living out marriage in their present relationships. In the case of marriage, it *is* possible to pour new wine into old wineskins without having the old wineskins torn asunder.

21

Steps to Recovering the Lost First Love

*I*t is usually in sexual matters that couples first sense something has gone wrong in their marriage. But we must not be so naive as to think that sexual inadequacies are necessarily the cause of marital deadness and the loss of passion. In most cases it's the other way around. Failure to establish exciting and intimate personal relationships in the ways a couple lives together, plays together, and has a common spiritual commitment has more to do with satisfaction in bed than what goes on in bed has to do with creating gratification in these crucial dimensions of life. Furthermore, if a couple makes a commitment to stay in their marriage, sexual passion can be recreated. This, I contend, can happen only if the husband and wife pay attention to how life out of bed is lived.

Of all the things that influence how we perform sexually, few are ever likely to prove more important than our jobs. Job fulfillment, or lack of it, has a powerful influence on marriage in general and on our sexual lives in particular. To ignore this reality is to fail to understand one of the most important factors contributing to passionate marriages.

A man whose job leaves him diminished and fails to provide him with the conviction that what he is doing is meaningful is likely to experience a noticeable decline in his libido level. The effect of having to spend most of his time each day in purposeless labor can cut back significantly on his appetite for sex. Blood tests reveal that the level of testosterone, the hormone that drives his sexuality, drops dramatically when a man's sense of worth and significance at the workplace is lessened. A wife ought to know this and recognize the signs. Her husband's loss of sexual interest may have nothing to do with any failure on her part to be sexually desirable. Instead it may be the direct consequence of what is happening to him in the workplace. A man whose personal identity and self-worth are being chipped away daily by those who control him in his vocational activities is not likely to have the self-assurance that good sex requires.

Making matters worse is that in the kind of world in which we live, a man whose job is destroying him probably won't even talk about his hurts. He will just withdraw. The fact that he was passed over for a promotion or not given the recognition he thought he deserved is not likely to be the sort of thing he shares, even with his wife. He is likely to cover up everything with bravado and try to give the impression he's king of the hill.

A deacon of a large Baptist church was publicly disgraced, asked to resign his position of church leadership, and eventually divorced by his wife as the result of being caught with a call girl in a cheap motel. His wife came to talk with me because she herself felt painfully humiliated by the whole affair. She was especially pained by the fact that over the past several months he had been rejecting her sexual interests in him while at the same time going to a prostitute to get his sexual gratification.

She just didn't understand how he could do that to her. As the full story of what had been going on came out, we learned that the bank where he had been a vice-president was merging with another bank and there was no room for him in the new organization. They were letting him stay on for a year out of kindness but, as a man made redundant, he had felt the condescending pity and lack of respect from people who had formerly been his employees. What made matters worse was that he no longer had any work to do that had any meaning to him or any significance for the bank. Overnight he had become an unnecessary piece of furniture that everyone wished would disappear.

All of this played itself out in the bedroom. His sense of inadequacy in the workplace eradicated his sense of masculinity. When he was with his wife he didn't feel man enough to perform sexually.

Making matters even worse was the fact that his wife, at the same time, was becoming a consciousness-raised new woman who believed she had the right to demand that her husband meet her sexual needs. There is nothing wrong with a wife expecting her desires and appetites to be satiated in a marriage; it was just that in this case the timing was all wrong. She was coming on strong just when he was feeling like nothing. He simply could not handle her new demands. His defense was to have arguments with her nightly over inconsequential concerns. He would then use the hostility of these arguments, which were often intense, as a means to ward off the possibility of having to do anything sexually.

What he did with that prostitute was by no means justifiable, but it was fully understandable why this hurting man did what he did. The prostitute, because she was a prostitute, did not seem to be his equal as a person. Comparatively, he did not feel like a failure when he was with her. Furthermore, she had no performance expectations for him. She had been with men like him before and knew how to be nonthreatening and to make him feel he was OK just the way he was. As he told me his story, it was clear that this experienced prostitute had made him feel like a man. He actually told me he had fallen in love with her. I can still hear him saying, "She meets my needs in ways my wife never did. If it weren't for her, I could never have survived."

Unfortunately, the "cure" he found with a prostitute was neither adequate nor lasting. A few months later that man hung himself in the toilet of a local bus station.

We live in the kind of world in which men who are threatened and emotionally emasculated often look for women whom they can *use* to bolster their faltering egos. And it is painfully true that there are women who, themselves, have been so hurt and diminished over the years that they are willing to be used like that. Thus we have scenarios in which wounded people create even greater tragedies in their lives and leave behind family and friends who have not the slightest idea as to why these tragedies happened.

We Need Creativity

It is imperative for us to realize that we are a people created in the image of a Creator, and that if our lives are devoid of creativity then we deny the essence of our humanity. Some people can find enough channels for creativity outside of the workplace. But they are often few and far between. For most of us, the jobs we go to from eight to five prove to be the most powerful agents either for energizing us to live life with passion or for leaving us so dissipated we have no taste for life at all.

A friend of mine is a happy example of how work can condition the passion in a marriage and the sexual fulfillment that partners get from each other. His wife had always come across to me as an uptight prude. She had been one of those persons I found difficult to be around. She had a deadening effect on any party and on any conversation. To say she was no fun would have been to be kind.

About a year ago my friend's wife took a job as a special education teacher. She had trained in college to work with mentally and physically handicapped children, but because of getting married and then getting pregnant she had never had the chance to do what she had always wanted to do.

After some professional counseling, she and her husband decided she needed to work and he needed to make the adjustments so she could do that. She was able to see the children off to school in the morning, and he changed his work hours so that he would be there when they came home at the end of the school day. He chipped in to help with the housework and laundry. He got into the shopping routine too. All at once this woman had a chance to do what she had dreamed of doing since her junior-high days.

The change in my friend's wife was more than remarkable; it was miraculous! Seemingly overnight she gained a whole new disposition. She became fun to talk to, and she suddenly seemed interested in everybody else. The deadness was gone and the sparkle to her personality made her radiate excitement.

I asked her husband if she had been to some kind of a Dale Carnegie course or had had some kind of religious conversion. He smiled, winked, and said, "If you think she's wild at a party, I can only say it's nothing to what she does to me when we're alone." It was fun just imagining.

In affecting a marriage, second to work is play. And the older I get, the more important play becomes in relationship to my capacity for passionate living. In my younger days I was consumed with what I was convinced was my God-given mission in life. Everything, I thought, hung on whether or not that mission was carried out effectively and totally. My wife and children were expected to understand my high calling and gratefully make the necessary sacrifice so I could carry out my life's mission.

But the years have passed, and the older I get the more convinced I am that God can save the world without me. Furthermore, my mission in life isn't all that matters. I am coming to realize that God has high callings for each of my family members too! My wife, for instance, who has become deeply committed to ending discrimination against all people regardless of race, religion, gender, or sexual orientation, now has embraced a mission for her life. I feel that what she is accomplishing may be more important right now than any of the things that I am trying to do.

But it is all too easy to get so consumed with our own sense of self-importance that we leave no time for fun. We are all too prone to take ourselves so seriously that there is no time left in our lives for play. That is why God gave us the Sabbath, and only people who are overwhelmed with a false consciousness of self-importance fail to observe it. Once a week God wants each of us to stop those hectic activities we deem so crucial and remember Him. He wants us to stop and acknowledge that He is God and not we, ourselves.

The Sabbath was not meant for the kind of somber observance practiced by our Puritan forefathers and foremothers. To be completely honest, I think those old New England patriarchs and matriarchs gave the whole notion of the Sabbath a bad name.

In Bible times people did not work on the Sabbath because it was a time of joyful celebration of all that God had created. As a matter of fact, coming to the temple at Jerusalem was anything but what we might call reverent. The God of creation is a God who creates joy and made His universe out of a playful heart. He is a God who wants His people to enter into His gates with songs that lift us up and get us dancing.

> And thou shalt eat before the LORD thy God, in the place which he shall choose to place his name there, the tithe of thy corn, of thy wine, and of thine oil, and the firstlings of thy herds and of thy flocks; that thou mayest learn to fear the LORD thy God always. . . . And thou shalt bestow that money for whatsoever thy soul lusteth after, for oxen, or for sheep, or for wine, or for strong drink, or for whatsoever thy soul desireth: and thou shalt eat there before the LORD thy God, and thou shalt rejoice, thou, and thine household. (Deut. 14:23, 26)

These days we had better learn how to play in a sanctified manner because we are being given more and more time to do just that. Unfortunately, as we move into this post-industrial era, people who do not know how to play also don't know what to do with their new leisure time. They are confused and usually go out and try to make work for themselves for no other reason than that they do not know how to do anything else.

Sex is a form of play. And, might I say, it's the best kind. I really have an argument with those uptight theologians who view it in other terms. Those kill-joy types of scholastic biblicists who want to make sex into something that is totally functional and designed only to perpetuate the human race turn me off, and they turn a lot of other people off too. No wonder so many with high libido levels have problems taking the church seriously or believing that the Christian faith can be freeing. Why can't those theologians see how important playing is in sex and how important it is in keeping us human and real? Why couldn't they grasp the all-too-obvious fact that the couple who play together stay together? And why couldn't they be honest enough to let us in on the fact that some of them enjoy sex and probably make a game of it from time to time?

But it's not just the theologians who are responsible for taking the fun out of sex. Some of the modern social scientists are to blame too. Those self-proclaimed enlightened psychologists and sociologists who write articles for magazines and appear on talk shows do a lot of the damage, even though they say their research is meant to help.

When I was in graduate school, I was given the assignment by my major professor, William F. Kephart, to survey the contents of the many sex manuals that were then flooding the market. He wanted me to see if there was any common theme to the writing and to find out if that special breed of social scientist we have come to call sexologists had any unified ideology or value system undergirding their work.

I must have waded through more than a dozen of those books. They had such enticing titles as *The Joy of Sex* and *Everybody Can Be Sexually Fulfilled*. The contents of the books were filled with careful instructions about almost anything and everything imaginable. There were specific directions as to what to eat prior to sexual relations, what kind of foreplay should be employed, and what positions to take before, during, and after the act.

Then it hit me! *These were books that made sex into work.* They made what was one of the last vestiges of spontaneity in an overly mechanized and controlled society into a highly disciplined activity. These books were job descriptions. They were prescriptions that told people how to do what was expected of them *right!* They made it all so serious. They made it hard to imagine anybody ever laughing in the midst of it all. The books reduced sexual play to a highly structured responsibility that demanded careful planning and explicit correctness. This is so wrong! Sex should be fun. And I am not about to say how to make it into fun, because then I would be doing just what those sexologists did. All that I can say is to make sure your partner is having a good time too. I believe God will be pleased with that.

Needless to say, there are many other kinds of play besides sexual play. It even can be argued that those who do not save some time and energy for play in everyday life apart from the bedroom won't have much to offer in the bedroom. Foreplay isn't just a physical thing. Sometimes it's a dressed-up night at the theater followed by a late dinner by candlelight. Often it requires the kind of meaningful conversation that makes one's partner into the most interesting person in the world.

Passionate marriages always require planning and imagination, but they don't always require a lot of money. A trip to the library with an old-fashioned walk home might turn the trick, or you might try a picnic dinner by moonlight at some special spot with a view. Don't let any accusations that you're being silly put you off. Married people need some craziness, and they certainly need to play. A word to the wise should be sufficient: If you don't play with your partner, don't be shocked if somebody else does. We were created to spend part of each day and part of each week at play, and if you don't provide the time and put forth the effort to make it happen, you are only setting up the conditions for somebody else to come along and make it happen.

22

Strange Encounters of a Wonderful Kind

Some years ago I asked my wife what she would like to do if I could give her an entire weekend for us to spend together. Because I'm on the speaking circuit and give high priority to church engagements, I don't often have any weekends to give away. I figured that such an offer would bring some exotic suggestion like a short trip to a luxury hotel in Bermuda. Instead, my wife said that more than anything else she wanted to go to a church-sponsored Marriage Encounter.

I had heard about the Marriage Encounter movement. I knew it had started with the Catholics and that it had since spread to mainline Protestant denominations. From what I had been told, I figured it helped people who felt their marriage needed some patching up or improving.

I told Peggy I thought our relationship seemed just fine to me and I didn't see that we had any real need to have some pseudo-guru marriage expert tamper with a good thing.

Peggy simply reminded me that I had offered to do anything *she* wanted to do and that the Marriage Encounter weekend was what she wanted to do more than anything. Besides, she pointed out, I was wrong about what the weekend was all about. It wasn't for people whose marriages were in trouble, but for people who had good marriages and felt they were so good and so gratifying that, more than anything else, they wanted to make them even better.

There really wasn't much that I could say after that. I mean, how could I argue against a wife who wanted more of a good thing? "And another thing," she pointed out, "the Marriage Encounter isn't led by a marriage counselor or psychotherapist anyway. It's led by a Catholic priest."

When I heard that, I no longer felt threatened. Since I wasn't a Catholic and we were going to a Catholic thing I was fairly sure nobody there would know me. Besides, there was nothing a priest sworn to celibacy was going to put over on me, or so I thought! So without further protest I said, "Sure!"

On the appointed Friday evening, we packed up the car and traveled a few miles down the road from our home to Chester, Pennsylvania, where we checked into a motel. If you know anything about Chester, you know it is not the sort of place that anybody could call romantic. And to tell the truth, I could think of a lot of places other than a Howard Johnson motel that could better serve as a setting for enriching a marriage. But a deal is a deal, and I did not say a word.

When the group of some twenty couples assembled the first evening, the priest in charge gave us some instructions and elicited some promises from us. He told us to take off our watches and put them away. From then on and until the end of the weekend, we were to make no attempt to keep track of the time. Furthermore, we were required to promise not to touch the television sets in our rooms. Personally I thought both of these requests were a bit too dramatic, but I complied.

Then each of us was given an eight-by-ten notebook and told we were going to be using it to write letters to each other. The priest went on to say that by the end of the weekend we would be given an hour and a half to write closing love letters to our mates—and that by then we would be complaining that it wasn't enough time.

Learning What's Important

With that last announcement, my skepticism reached new limits. I thought to myself, *If this guy had any idea what I am like, he would know I can hardly fill a postcard when I write home to my wife from a road trip.*

There were some other directions, like not being able to talk to anyone other than your own marital partner and keeping the shades in your room drawn at all times.

I'm not going to tell you all that was actually said and done on our weekend. All that I feel is necessary is to say that we had the opportunity to hear from people who had been on Marriage Encounter weekends before. Couples told how *their* lives had been changed. People shared some important realizations they had made about themselves and each other and the transitions in their lives that had come about as a result of it all. And I have to admit that I, who am easily bored and have a hard time sitting still in one place for any length of time, was almost mesmerized by what they said.

But what made the greatest impression on me was not the talk; it was the writing in that notebook that I received upon arrival. After careful instructions, I was asked to write to my wife describing such things as:

When was the time I felt closest to you?

When was the time you hurt me the most?

What is it about you that I find desirable?

What is there about myself that I have never shared with you and want to?

With each of these questions Peggy and I would separate from each other for about an hour to write, then just the two of us would get together in our room, exchange books, and read what the other had to say. Then we talked things over for another hour. We did that over and over with each of the questions.

As the weekend unfolded, both of us were amazed by how many important things there were in our lives that we had not known before and how little we had been sharing ourselves with one another over the past few years. I had always thought we communicated well with each other, but over that weekend we both realized that our talk had been mostly chatter and that a host of deep feelings, both good and bad, had gone unexpressed in our relationship. In so many ways we discovered in those two and a half days that we had, to some degree, unconsciously become somewhat distant toward one another. I knew the Peggy that I had married, but I had been too busy to get to know the one who had been evolving since that day long ago when we took our vows.

With the discoveries we were making about each other, there was a growing excitement about being with each other. All the taken-for-grantedness that had crept into our relationship seemed to have vanished. This woman was still my wife, yet she seemed new to me and offered the intrigue that only newness can offer. I was feeling a depth to our relationship that I had almost forgotten was possible. And there was passion!! It was intense! It was real! It was good!

And yes, one of the last things we did before we went home from the weekend was to write each other love letters. And yes, just like that priest had told us, an hour and a half was not enough time to do it.

I would like for every married couple to go on a Marriage Encounter weekend. It is easy enough to arrange. The pastor or priest of your local church probably knows how to set up such an experience for you right there in your own neck of the woods. And if you can't get any help from your minister or priest, you can call the national headquarters of the Marriage Encounter movement and get the name of someone nearby who can help you to get involved in this special kind of experience.

Marriage Encounter
1908 E. Highland, #A
San Bernardino, California 92404
909-881-3456 or 800-795-LOVE

Being realistic, I know that most of those who read this won't go on a Marriage Encounter weekend for one reason or another. But if you can't, you should know there are things you can do for your marriage on your own. You can commit yourself to living out the basic principles that undergird Marriage Encounter weekends, even if you don't go on one. These principles are not unique to this movement or even particularly new. Solid relationships and passionate marriages have always been built on these principles. Furthermore, they are principles that were lived out in Jesus and were the ground upon which he built a passionate lifestyle that all who follow after Him seek to imitate.

First, take time to pay attention. Jesus was never too busy to listen and to learn what was going on in people's lives. Whether it was listening to a woman by a well or sitting down with a demoniac in a cemetery, Jesus seemed always ready to stop everything and pay deep attention to what those He loved wanted to share about themselves. His empathetic manner enabled Him to not only hear what people had to say to Him, but also to discern what they really meant. The two are not always the same. Jesus reached out as He listened and felt His way into other people's hearts and souls. It is not surprising that the Bible says He "knew their thoughts" (Matt. 12:25).

Once, some years ago, a student came to my office after a lecture and asked me a rather perfunctory question. As he sat there asking me something about some theory I had expounded in class, I was a bit impatient. I had other things I had to do. He could have looked up the answer himself, and I was really a bit too busy right then to give him any real quality time.

That young man left my office, returned to the high-rise apartment house where he lived, went up to the roof, and jumped to his death. His life was snuffed out less than twenty minutes after he had left me.

I was the last one to ever talk to that young man. I now realize that when he came to my office, it wasn't to ask a question about sociology, but to cry out for help. He had heard me speak with passion about love during class and probably had been led to believe that I cared for him. He reached out, and in my busyness I heard only what he said. I did not hear his feelings. I missed the cry for help that often comes over and under the words of troubled people. I failed to hear what this young man meant; I did not grasp what he could not put into words. Jesus would have done better.

What I failed to do for that young man I find that husbands and wives often fail to do for each other; they don't stop everything else when it's time to listen and pay attention to each other's souls. So many married people do not seem to understand how important it is to regularly take time to feel these groanings that cannot be uttered (see Rom. 8:26).

Second, be willing to share your secrets. Jesus was! In the Bible we find that He did not withhold the truths about Himself from those who were near and dear to Him. He said to His disciples:

> "Henceforth I call you not servants; for the servant knoweth not what his lord doeth: but I have called you friends; for all things that I have heard of my Father I have made known unto you." (John 15:15)

So often, I, unlike Jesus, keep things from the one whom I like to say is my best friend—my wife. They are sometimes things that embarrass me, and I am silent because I think she might be hard on me and make me feel worse. This, of course, is nothing more than a lack of trust.

Sometimes I say nothing because I don't think Peggy will understand. This constitutes a lack of faith in her capacity to sympathize with me.

And sometimes I keep my secrets just because I'm too busy to go through the hassle of unburdening myself to her. If I am honest I have to admit that this treats her as though she's just not very important to me.

All of these attitudes and dispositions are unloving, and the more they are lived out, the less we have to say to each other and the more the passion dies. Every married person ought to declare war on them and try to banish them. The gospel is a call to discover a kind of love that will set such things behind us and press on to the high calling of God in Christ Jesus our Lord (Phil. 3:14). Consider these verses:

> [Love] beareth all things, believeth all things, hopeth all things, endureth all things. (1 Cor. 13:7)
>
> [Love] shall cover the multitude of sins. (1 Pet. 4:8)
>
> Perfect love casteth out fear. (1 John 4:18)
>
> [Love] never faileth. (1 Cor. 13:8)

Realizing these truths should make us willing and ready to be open and honest with each other and to share our secrets.

Third, always be ready to express your love. Jesus was. His ultimate love letter was being nailed to a cross. Love has to be *expressed* if it is to impact another person. What is most surprising is that the more we express it, the more intense love becomes. Love is nurtured to greatness in its expression. Jesus' love for us grows more intense daily because every day He shows us His love and reaches out to us in multiple and usually obvious ways. Certainly, in His forgiveness of us Jesus expresses His love for us. Long ago He told us this story just to make that point:

> "There was a certain creditor which had two debtors: the one owed five hundred pence, and the other fifty. And when they had nothing to pay, he frankly forgave them both. Tell me therefore, which of them will love him most? Simon answered and said, I suppose that he, to whom he forgave the most. And he said unto him, Thou hast rightly judged. And he turned to the woman, and said unto Simon, Seest thou this woman? I entered into thine house, thou gavest me no water for my feet: but she hath washed my feet with tears, and wiped them with the hairs of her head." (Luke 7:41–43)

What Jesus revealed in this story is something all married persons have to learn in the everyday rounds of their lives together. They need to know that we grow in love with each other to the extent that we do loving things for each other. And the most loving thing we can do is to express loving forgiveness daily.

Our actions create our feelings even more than our feelings create our actions. To increase passion in a marital relationship, therefore, is fully within the domain of the will. When this lesson is learned we make a major transition. Immature people think that passion only comes by surprise. They think it is something they have no control over. That, of course, would be sad if it were true. Were that the case, when passion ebbed out of our lives, we would be helpless to bring it back. But the good news is that there is much we can do through a determination of the will to control and make it ever more powerful. That is why the apostle Paul so perfectly tells us:

> When I was a child, I spake as a child, I understood as a child, I thought as a child: but when I became a man, I put away childish things. (1 Cor. 13:11)

When it comes to love, most adults have a deeper understanding than young people, even though young people, for the most part, think they understand and feel love better than anybody else. In their child-ishness young people think passion just "happens" if the right romantic object is available. We are grown up when we recognize that passion is within our will to create it.

Keeping a Promise

One of the most remarkable stories of passion created by the will concerns a man called Robertson McQuilken. As a young man, he dreamed of becoming the president of Columbia Bible College in Columbia, South Carolina. He adored his father, who had held this po-sition, and he aspired to someday take his father's place.

Robertson McQuilken's dream came true. One day he did become the president of Columbia Bible College. When he took that position, he sensed an affirmation and a powerful call from God. This position was his, he knew, not just because he wanted it, but because God had called him to it.

Dr. McQuilken served as president of Columbia Bible College for a number of years and did so with distinction. He led Columbia to be-come a premier Christian institution that has prepared hundreds of young people for service, both in the United States and overseas.

Then one day this very special man realized he had a tragedy on his hands. His wife began to show the symptoms of Alzheimer's disease. This was no slow-moving case, and in a matter of months there were dramatic consequences. She not only lost the memory of much of their life together, but she was unable to even recognize him. She lost all awareness that he was her husband.

Robertson McQuilken made his decision. He resigned the presidency of Columbia so he could give full-time care to his wife. Without hesitation he walked away from his calling as an act of love for her.

There were realists who told him there was no point to what he was doing. Anybody could take care of his poor wife, they told him, but not anybody could be president of Columbia Bible College. And after all, she didn't even recognize him when he came into the room to help her.

Then there were pious critics who brought up the fact that he was walking away from a calling from God. He was letting his personal concern for his wife interfere with his service to the Lord, they said.

The man's answers were magnificent. To the realists he readily admitted that his wife didn't know who he was. But that wasn't the point, he told them. *The really important thing was that he still knew who she was* and, furthermore, he let them know that he recognized in her now-forgetful self the same lovely woman he had married those many years ago.

Then he turned to the pious critics. His words to them were even more profound: "There is only one thing more important than a calling. And that is a promise. And I promised to be there for her 'until death do us part.'"

Do not pity Robertson McQuilken. He is not the victim of a marriage that no longer has passion in it. If you think he is, you are wrong. This is a man who has created passion through a decision to express his love and who maintains it by a sheer commitment of the will. As he sits with his wife and cares for her, we might even envy him. I am convinced that his heart still reaches out to her. Perhaps now more than ever.

You, too, can make it happen. There is no esoteric technique for creating and maintaining passion in marriage. What I learned in that Marriage Encounter in Chester were principles that any student of the art of loving will validate.

You have to take time to pay attention. You have to share your innermost secrets about how you feel and what is happening in your life.

And you have to find special ways to express your love, because love must be given away if it is to be kept.

Passion in marriage is as simple and as difficult as all of that.

PART IX

COMING ALIVE WHILE
MAKING A LIVING

23

This Job Is Killing Me

*A*s I have already said, some people go to work and die. Their jobs seem devoid of anything that resembles fulfillment. Many women and men feel like what they do for a living doesn't amount to much, and their lives are going nowhere. They look with envy at people who seem to do things the world considers significant and who get to realize their potential (as they say on "Donahue"). They feel trapped, and they sense the energy of their lives ebbing away.

Some of them are people who know they have had their chances. But somehow they never seemed able to launch out into the deep. Perhaps the timing wasn't right. Or it may have been that there were other commitments. Maybe there were car payments and the kids' tuition bills. There were good reasons, very good reasons, why they gave up on the dream and settled instead for the security that goes with staying put. But when they did, something in them died. Or maybe it was just that they left something of themselves back there in that moment when they turned their backs on the risk and let the dream slip away.

These people hurt a lot, but it's not an intense pain. It is not the sort of pain that great authors depict in plays and novels. This pain doesn't create existential despair. Instead it is hardly noticeable, only felt when they sit alone in stillness or go to high-school reunions.

The Blackwood Brothers sang about some of the things I am describing when they recorded Don and Harold Reid's song called "The Class of '57":

> Tommy's sellin' used cars,
> Nancy's fixin' hair,
> Harvey runs a groc'ry store
> And Marg'ret doesn't care;
> Jerry drives a truck for Sears
> And Charlotte's on the make,
> And Paul sells life insurance
> And part-time real estate.
>
> And the Class of Fifty-Seven had its dreams.
> But we all thought we'd change the world
> With our great works and deeds;
> Or maybe we just thought
> The world would change to fit our needs.
> The Class of Fifty-Seven had its dreams.
>
> Betty runs a trailer park,
> Jan sells Tupperware,
> Randy's in an insane ward,
> And Mary's on welfare;
> Charley took a job with Ford,
> Joe took Freddy's wife,
> Charlotte took a millionaire,
> And Freddy took his life.
>
> And the Class of Fifty-Seven had its dreams.
> But livin' life from day to day
> Is never like it seems.

Things get complicated
When you get past eighteen,
But the Class of Fifty-Seven had its dreams.
Ah, the Class of Fifty-Seven had its dreams.

It really isn't too difficult to evade the consciousness of this kind of emptiness in life. Television is one common escape, but there are plenty of other distractions. Some of these escape artists become avid sports fans because they find excitement in the exploits of others. They feel a vicarious excitement when their team wins a World Series or a Super Bowl. They find they can lose themselves in these games. Somehow they can see themselves as winners if their teams win, and they sense bitterness and defeat if their teams don't win.

Women's organizations concerned with abuse have been sending out warnings across the country so that wives can brace themselves for what can happen following the final whistle on a Super Bowl Sunday. They know that men whose team has been defeated sometimes react by brutalizing their wives. Knowing what could happen on such days, shelters for battered women prepare for a rush of clients.

For far too many men whose everyday lives hold little emotional satisfaction, "the big game" is not a game at all. It is what these men live for. A loss by their favorite team has powerful implications for them that those of us who are not so psychologically involved cannot possibly comprehend.

One of the sad commentaries of our time is that American men are increasingly becoming couch potatoes. So many men are escaping the deadness of their lives through vicarious participation in sports that watching games on TV has become a national pastime. Having benched themselves and disengaged from anything that might give their lives invigorating significance, more and more men have become resigned to simply watching the exploits of athletic celebrities. Jocks are becoming surrogates for living. Charles Barkley, the somewhat outspoken superstar of the Phoenix Suns basketball team, complained that he's "just a player" and that people have no right to expect him to live up to their expectations of him in private life. Poor Charles did not realize when he made that statement that he isn't paid those millions of dollars just to score baskets. He has to realize he is being paid to be a substitute for men all across America who have lost confidence in their own ability to live heroically. To many of his fans, Charles Barkley is not just a player. He's an alter ego.

The sports escape is not an exclusively male phenomenon. Indeed, many women are into it too. But women, for the most part, have carved out their own special instrument for vicarious escape from lives devoid of passionate aliveness. Women have discovered soap operas.

When I was a kid, there were soap operas on the radio, but they did not have the psychological hold on women that the TV soaps have today. Back then, women would listen to the soaps on the radio while they did other things. But with the television soaps, total surrender and complete involvement is required. Each weekday afternoon millions of women stop everything to give their complete attention to this world of make-believe. Married to men who, in many instances, have made sex an expression and extension of their emotionally and psychically barren lives, these women look to the usually sordid experiences of fictitious characters for some psycho-sexual release.

It wasn't supposed to be like this. They married with the expectation that life was going to be rich with feeling. They had been brought up on the myth that sharing life with "the right person" would give them all that life is supposed to give anyone. For them love was not going to be the empty shell they had seen it become for others. They knew all about those older couples in restaurants who sit with shoulders drooped in deadly silence waiting for food that bores them as much as they bore each other. And they made up their minds this would *never* happen to them. Theirs would be the great love that would last forever. That simple lifestyle of dusting, vacuuming, and cooking was going to be more than enough for their happiness if it just carried with it a relationship of passion.

For most of the homemakers who believed the myth, it didn't turn out to be that way. Each woman had a story that went something like this: Her husband's work diminished his humanity, and his spirit was dissipated in the workplace. He returned home to his wife as the "hollow man, the empty man." When she asked what went on at work he simply answered, "Nothing." And "nothing" was what happened when he was with her too. Then one day she took a break and watched a little TV and found something that reminded her of what might have been.

There they were—lovers with passion. Life filled with intrigue and passion. People who were linked with people in ways that mattered desperately. And the sex was full of passion too. It was lurid and dangerously exciting. It was marked by the fantasies she had of love too great to be confined by bourgeois convention and the rules that order most of our lives. These people on the soaps would never settle for the life she was living. They risked disgrace and even the rejection of their own children to be in the arms of one who seemed to make them feel fully alive. And so she watched the soaps and dreamed her dreams.

A friend of mine who pastors a church told me a story that falls into the category of theater known as black comedy. At his church's weekly prayer meeting, a woman in his congregation asked if the other church members would remember in prayer one of the characters in the show "As the World Turns." My friend told me, "She was serious! She was dead serious. The make-believe character in her soap opera had become more real to her than the people in her own family. She was more involved with the problems of someone in a soap opera than she was in the real sufferings of people she lived with day in and day out." Such escapes from the passionless mundane might be funny to watch if they were not so pitifully sad.

But not everybody gets sucked into these absurdities. Some folks out there refuse to play these kinds of games for the simple reason that they find no escape through such harmless amusements. Neither the characters in television dramas nor the bigger-than-life players in the ball games give them sufficient deliverance from the gnawing feelings of insignificance they have about themselves or the deadness of their lives. These are dangerous people because they seek escape in dangerous ways. Some of them hit the bottle. Others try drugs. Many of them become suicidal, and some lead criminal lives. But for many of these sad people the response to an existence without passion is simply to drop out.

Dropping out has always been an alternative. In the 1930s we called those who chose this route of escape *hobos*. Unlike *bums*, who might be people with drinking problems or just plain lazy folks, hobos were people who simply ran away from it all. They rode the freight cars to bask in the Florida sun, and they traveled to the likes of New York and Chicago, weather permitting. They were the free spirits idealized by Woody Guthrie's songs. They were the people who refused to be boxed in and buried by the system.

In the fifties we called these dropouts *beatniks*, and we often traveled to Greenwich Village in New York just to hear their poetry and watch them loll around.

In the early sixties, we called them *hippies*, or *flower children*. They reacted to the Vietnam War, not with ideological protests, but with disinterest. They were into love and community and did not see any sense in fighting in a war that was supposed to save a social system they had already rejected.

Nowadays there are more respectable types of dropouts. We find them in the hills of Vermont and in the mountains of Colorado, and sometimes we come across them sleeping out on the beaches of Hawaii. Occasionally they build energy-efficient houses with earthen roofs, and some of them float into the New Age colonies. But the dropouts are still with us, and I suppose they always will be.

I think that all of us establishment types have times when we look at the dropouts with a certain degree of envy. When life seems to be too much for us to handle, when the endless details of taking care of things gang up on us, when the bureaucratic pressures that go with our jobs seem to make no sense at all, who doesn't think how nice it would be just to walk away from it all and go to never-never land? I suppose I might have done it if I didn't believe that "none of us liveth to himself, and no man dieth to himself" (Rom. 14:7).

I don't think I could live with myself if I just walked away from my life when I felt myself drowning in it. It would be too selfish of an answer. When I saw the movie *Kramer vs. Kramer,* I think I had some feel for why the wife and mother felt she had to just up and leave her family. Meryl Streep, who played this desolate woman, convinced the audience that to stay was to die. But as the story unfolded, I, along with the rest of the audience, gradually turned against her. And when she returned a couple of years later to reclaim her child, we were all against her.

"You just don't walk out and leave others to struggle without you," I said to myself. "In the long run, that kind of response to a lifestyle that eats away at the soul is too selfish."

"No man is an island," wrote John Donne. He also said, "Never send to know for whom the bell tolls; it tolls for thee."

We are responsible for others, and our personal salvation can never be justified if we simply walk away from them and the debts we owe them.

That doesn't mean people ought never to walk away from jobs that deaden their souls. Many people have demonstrated that one can drop out with responsibility and dignity.

I once knew a Christian couple who didn't find much gratification in their roles as teachers. They were employed by a wealthy suburban school district, and the kids they taught seemed spoiled and overly preoccupied with how wonderful they were. Other Christian teachers seemed to have a heart for these "with-it" high-schoolers, but for this particular couple the students came across as plastic and selfishly demanding. So one day they picked up themselves and their children and moved to a small South Seas island in Micronesia. There they spent their days reaching out to boys and girls who seemed open to their love and who, themselves, had a great capacity for loving back.

I know a corporate executive who dropped out of his San Francisco business firm and became a full-time builder with Habitat for Humanity. Today he's building houses for poor people in Third World countries. He and his family have reestablished their lives at the edge of a Latin American barrio.

The last thing this man would say is that he acted irresponsibly. He claims that he rescued his family from the devastating effects of the affluent American lifestyle and its preoccupation with things. He believes his children are better off in an environment where it is more important to have friends than to have things. And he is positively convinced that his energies are better spent building houses for and

with poor families than they ever were in shuffling papers on the fifti-
eth floor of a corporate skyscraper.

If it were necessary to convince you, I could easily make out a long
list of people who dropped out of lifestyles that were killing their souls
and stifling their enthusiasm for life. These people dared to drop out
and venture into new roles that provide little security but have great
potential for passionate living. I could give you the details of a former
congressman who is now working in an urban settlement house. And
there's the story of a bank president who quit a job with a six-figure
salary to teach math in an inner-city school. And I know if I asked
around, I could come up with hundreds of other stories like these.

There are responsible ways to drop out of these dehumanizing roles
that are sapping the life out of us. And there are alternatives to what
seems to many of us to be jobs that destroy our capacity for passion. I
want to go on to affirm that for many, such a route out of deadness is
the only way to go.

In *The Great Escape Isn't Always Necessary*, T. S. Eliot, perhaps the
most important English poet of the twentieth century, tried to help us
to understand that there is a way of leaving our absurd and deadening
lives without ever leaving home. For many of us who seek that place
where life can be lived with meaning and passion, it is a remarkable
discovery to learn that we can "at the end of all our exploring, return
to the same place we began and to know it for the first time."

Such a possibility rings with hope for those of us who cannot sail
to some South Seas island or follow a vision to work with Mother
Teresa. That this hope was articulated by a poet whose writings ex-
plored the passionless existence of people like us makes his words all
the more promising.

It was T. S. Eliot who wrote in his famous poem "The Love Song
of J. Alfred Prufrock":

> In the room the women come and go
> Talking of Michelangelo.

That couplet struck me to heart when I first read it, and it got me
thinking on the theme that has become the theme of this book. As I

read it, I thought of those people at the afternoon tea who knew nothing of the passionate life of the great Michelangelo, discussing him as a form of sophisticated, escapist entertainment. Having no capacity to live out the passion of the ultimate Renaissance man, they had resigned themselves to reducing his agony and ecstasy to drawing-room prattle.

When a man like T. S. Eliot, who could scathingly denounce the superficiality of citizens in Western societies, suggests that it is possible to achieve a new awareness of life without dropping out or "leaving home," I think we have to pay attention. We have to ask how this is possible. And, most important, we have to be ready to take the steps to make it happen.

I believe we should focus our attention in this quest on our relationships to the people who are around us. It is in these relationships that we can have our first taste of real aliveness as well as receive the energy to enter into all the other arenas of our lives with passionate appreciation.

Even as I say this, there may be some wary traditionalists who wonder if, in this approach, I am leaving the confines of orthodox Christianity. Nothing could be further from the truth. If there is one thing I want to make clear, it is that being "in Christ" is the *only* basis for experiencing the resurrection from deadness. Christ *is* the answer! What I want us to do is to consider the means Christ usually uses to bring His answer into play. I want us to look to Scripture for guidance as to how to actualize the new humanity we seek that we might have hitherto overlooked or minimized.

To be right up-front, I say here and now that I believe Christ has chosen to pour His life-giving presence into us through those brothers and sisters we encounter all too casually in our everyday lives. I am going to try to show how the ordinary people we talk and work with in the common affairs of life provide a continual possibility for a *theophany*. I believe the place where you work for some forty hours a week to earn your living can be redefined as holy ground where you can stand ready to experience the glory of God. If you have eyes to see and ears to hear, you can discover in the workplace a whole new level of experiencing life.

I was almost reluctant to use the word *theophany* because it is one of those highfalutin words that is not likely to be a part of most people's vocabulary. In fact, it's not even in most dictionaries. A theophany is a breakthrough of the transcendent into the mundane. It is an ordinary event in the world that suddenly takes on supernatural meaning. No other word quite says what theophany means.

A Theophany in the Workplace

I belong to a labor-management team that goes by the name "The Value of the Person" (VOP). That name does a good job of conveying what this team wants to achieve as we try to bring union leaders and management personnel together for honest and meaningful dialogue. Our goal is to try to get people to value one another. We work hard to get those who are usually cast in adversarial roles to look beyond the labels they assign to each other and to relate to one another as sacred persons. We endeavor to help a shop steward look into the face of a plant manager and, instead of seeing an enemy who triggers his defenses, see a person who can be loving and who waits to be loved. Likewise, we want managers to be able to see their employees as individuals and friends instead of "labor" to be exploited. "The Value of the Person" works with secular corporations for the most part, but our team is nevertheless overtly Christian. We utilize the relationship models we find in the Scripture as models to be replicated in modern business and in the workplace.

Surprising things happen at our VOP seminars. For instance, one afternoon one of the members of our team, a former president of a union local of the United Steel Workers named Lefty Scumaci, was having a somewhat frustrating time. Then, without thinking, he blurted out to those at the seminar the simple declaration, "You know, everything would change if you guys would just treat one another like the other person was Jesus."

It wasn't a particularly overpowering revelation. In all probability the people in attendance had heard something like that before in some church service or religious rally. But sometimes timing is what makes truth work. And evidently the timing for this statement couldn't have been better. It seemed to have a startling effect. A simple statement, which probably had been heard before by all of these people, seemed in that moment to be really heard for the first time.

Something happened! An insight took hold! A conversion was taking place, and everyone there could feel it.

Later our team went back to visit that same company. It is our practice to stage a follow-up dinner a year or so after each of our consulting seminars so we can get from the participants a sense of what impact the seminar might have had on their workplace. We usually get good reports at these dinners, but on this particular evening the testimonies were extravagant. Labor leaders and managers talked about the friendships they had formed. There were jokes that went back and forth, and somebody said, "If you think this is fun, you should be with us Monday mornings at the shop."

I watched people who had previously regarded each other as enemies now talking to each other as brothers and sisters. There was even some hugging going on. But the most telling story of all came from a worker who told me, "When my boss's kid was sick and in the hospital, I went and saw him every day on the way home from work. I would've never done that before, but I just knew how much it would mean to him if I stopped by. That boy of his is a great kid, and I really liked getting to know him and hear him tell stories about his old man."

That shop a year earlier had been described as a "rotten place to have to work." In just a year it had become a place of fun and deep sharing. All because people started treating one another as though the other was Jesus.

As I took in the stories, I could not help but remember an old Hasidic Jewish tale about a rabbi and an abbot of a monastery who often took walks with each other in the woods. Each of them looked forward to these special times because each found in the other a sympathetic listener to the problems faced daily in carrying out his respective religious responsibilities.

One day the abbot confessed that there had been a rash of conflicts in the monastery. He told how the monks had become petty and were constantly being mean to each other. "As a matter of fact," said the abbot, "unless something changes, I fear the fellowship of the monastery will fall apart and nobody will want to come and be a part of our community."

"This is very strange news," responded the rabbi, "especially since it is widely rumored that one of your monks is the Messiah."

When the abbot returned to his monastery, he reported to the brothers the incredible thing the rabbi had told him. Everyone was abuzz about this news and everyone wondered which of them might be the holy one. Each looked upon the other with an inquisitive manner. Each wondered whether the brother he met in the daily round of work could be the Christ, living among them.

It is said that in the days that followed, all bickering and complaining ceased. Furthermore, the spiritual life of the monks was quickly raised to a brilliantly high level. And word of the love and of the quality of life at the monastery spread far and wide. Instead of declining, the fellowship of the brothers grew in number and increased in spiritual depth. And all of this happened because of a rumor that suggested, "the Messiah is among you!"

The Workplace as a Place for Character Formation

Making the workplace into a holy place where one finds encounters of love is essential for the character formation of the people who work there. In today's world what happens in the marketplace and in the factory is probably even more important spiritually than what happens in the church. This might offend some of the clergy, but it is nevertheless empirically true.

People spend forty hours a week at their jobs while they only spend an hour or so a week at church. The relationships we develop at work are often deeply personal while, in contrast, the relationships we form at church are often necessarily limited by time constraints. Our values, attitudes, and outlook on life are more likely to be formed by what goes on at work than by what goes on in a Sunday school class or even at a morning worship service. And finally, commitments to our jobs almost always take precedence over our commitments to church membership. Consider the likelihood of a person refusing to move to another part of the country when ordered to do so by an employer on the grounds that such a move would sever his or her church ties. That does happen sometimes, I suppose, but it just doesn't happen very often.

The bad news is that as important in character formation as the workplace proves to be for most people, most of them do not have a happy time there. Paul Goodman, the famous linguist and social commentator, estimated that as many as 82 percent of American workers don't like being at work and can't wait to be freed from what work does to them. That's the bad news. The good news is that it doesn't have to be that way.

The workplace can be redeemed. It can be transformed from a place where people slowly lose their humanity into vital communities of friendships that feed people's souls and give to them a joy they can carry out into the rest of the world, especially back to their families and churches. Such a thing will not happen easily. But it can and sometimes does happen. And making it happen is something we can learn.

24

Community in the Workplace

I contend that if churches want to be more effective in ministering to people and in helping them have spiritually fulfilling lives, they will recognize what jobs are doing to people and do everything possible to help create humanizing communities in the workplace. It can be argued that the socially relevant churches of the twentieth century will be those that discover ways to show how Jesus and the work of the Holy Spirit can play themselves out in offices and factories. Such churches will recognize the workplaces as the contemporary sector of everyday life where a person's character is established. It is in the workplace that church members will either live as Christians or be absorbed into a secular lifestyle.

This task will prove to be difficult in our pluralistic society where respecting other people's belief systems is essentially the right thing to do. That means our evangelization of people into the kind of humanizing relationships prescribed by the New Testament must be done with great care and without any kind of coercion. If Christians are to be "leaven" in the workplace, we must find ways for non-Christians to experience the benefits of a humanizing community without necessarily becoming believers in Jesus.

It is encouraging to note that the Bible more than supports this kind of cooperation and positive fellowship with those who are not in our own particular theological camp. In the Scriptures we regularly read about how "God-fearing men" and those committed to biblical faith had no difficulty in attempting to create together a just and kind social space for others to live in. Christians shouldn't be afraid of cooperative spiritual community. They will find that such ventures can sometimes bring about conversions to Christ. When God-fearing people experience the kind of community God wills for the workplace, they become open to a personal relationship with God through Christ. Those who join in and work along with Christians to change the workplace so that it expresses more justice and love often discover the essence of the gospel. To illustrate this, let me tell you about what happened to Ralph Smith, a friend of mine from the sixties.

Ralph and I worked together in the fair housing movement, that part of the civil rights movement that sought to make all housing available to all people, regardless of race, creed, or nationality. He came from a Quaker background, and while he believed in the ethical teachings of Jesus he would not have considered himself to have had what we evangelicals call a born-again experience. But in his attempt to bring about open housing in the suburban communities surrounding Philadelphia, Ralph was willing to be allied with several of us who were evangelical Christians. Our commitment to social justice was fed by our personal relationship with Christ and legitimated by Scriptures. Ralph had not, up until that time, had any close associations with people who thought that way or lived like that.

The sense of unity we evangelicals felt with Ralph as we worked with him and followed his wise counsel soon became both deep and dynamic. As we struggled with issues, tried to heal one another's wounds, and sought spiritual guidance in establishing strategies for action, little by little Ralph became infected with our faith.

I met Ralph several years later in a worship service at a charismatic church where I was to be a speaker. His hands were raised in worship. He radiated the joy of a person in love with Jesus. And it was obvious that Ralph was very much into the mystical dimensions of a personal relationship with Christ.

When I talked with him after the service I was very pleased to discover that he had lost none of his zeal for seeking social justice for the oppressed. As a matter of fact, he seemed more radically committed to social activism than ever. As I have watched Ralph since his personal encounter with Christ, I have found him to be the most striking example I know of a person evangelized into a personal relationship with Christ by working for justice in the context of Christian fellowship.

Ralph experienced the presence of Christ in a group that shared his humanistic commitment to justice, and once having tasted of that presence, he wanted to know its source. We never laid the evangelistic message on him in words, but Ralph experienced the presence of the resurrected Jesus as He moved in the midst of some brothers and sisters who shared His Spirit of love.

Community in House-Building

Over the past few years, I have been heavily involved with Habitat for Humanity, an organization that seeks to provide decent housing for poor people. In villages and cities around the world, Habitat for Humanity brings together concerned people who volunteer labor and money to build homes for those who, under ordinary circumstances, could never expect to own homes of their own. This organization, though created by Christians and established on Christian principles, has been open to people who do not necessarily share in the evangelical faith or express their concerns in Christian language. The non-evangelical participants are usually sincere and good people who have a heart for the poor. They are living out a high humanistic creed that translates into doing good for others.

When Habitat workers team up together to build houses, they often experience a sense of community that runs deeper than what is commonly known in most church gatherings. There sometimes emerges from their common labor a unified spirit and a feeling of shared values that binds them together, regardless of their religious backgrounds.

Participants in Habitat projects inevitably testify as to how the transforming power of the community that they discovered in building houses changed them. They frequently explain that their perspectives on everything from politics and economics to the meaning of friendship and spirituality were affected. People who were not Christians have been changed into new persons in Christ through their Habitat relationships, and for some Christians, involvement has led to what they sometimes refer to as a second conversion.

Some people are skeptical about the possibility of creating spiritual community in the secular workplace. My illustrations thus far have been about how Christian community has been created in organizations and with groups that were created to work for social justice and to eliminate the problems of the poor and oppressed. There are those who would argue that in factories and offices governed by the economic necessities of profit-making, such community would not be so easy to create. They would contend that the kind of spiritual idealism I have been describing is impossible to work out in a purely commercial setting. While I agree that it is not easy, I know it can be done; it *is* being done.

In Philadelphia one of the most brilliant examples of what I am talking about can be found in Cardone Industries. Some years ago Michael Cardone and his father started a business in which they "remanufacture" automobile parts. They get parts from junked automobiles, take them apart, clean them up, and put them together again so they are like new. They do this with engines, carburetors, transmissions, clutches, and a number of other car parts. Their remanufactured parts are sold around the world at relatively low prices, making it possible for people to get major repairs for their cars at more affordable prices. I think this is a good business for a Christian to be in. But it is in the workplace itself that Cardone Industries does its best work for the kingdom of God. There, effective measures have been taken, not only to provide good jobs for Cardone employees, but to create an atmosphere of caring and joy.

I visited Cardone Industries early one Thursday when I had been invited to speak at the company's 7:30 A.M. chapel service. Each day of work at Cardone Industries begins with a worship and testimony time.

That morning the chapel, which could hold about two hundred people, was about half-filled. That was about one-third of the more than three hundred workers employed at the plant. I was impressed, considering the fact that those who did attend did so on their own time and had to get up an hour earlier in order to be there.

The crowd was ethnically mixed because Michael Cardone makes a special effort to employ minority people who have difficulty finding jobs. About a third of the group were Puerto Ricans, and another third were recent Asian immigrants. Cardone Industries employs several bilingual chaplains who provide an evangelistic outreach to these workers and also serve as translators for those employees who do not have a good grasp of English. Two churches in the neighborhood near Cardone Industries have been organized by these chaplains, and each church has a core group of people who have been drawn together in the workplace.

The morning chapel I attended began with gospel singing; then several workers gave personal testimonies as to what Jesus was doing in their lives and how the friends they had made at work had turned out to be the best friends they had ever had. The service had a strong charismatic flavor. There was hand-clapping and smiles everywhere. I had a hard time believing such religious enthusiasm could happen so early in the morning.

Following the service I went out on the floor of the plant, and what I saw there was equally impressive. At 8:30 A.M. the work day started by having the employees gather in groups of ten to talk together and, for those who wanted to, to pray. In these team gatherings, the workers talked about any problems they might be having either on the job or in their lives outside the plant. During the prayer time, those who were not into praying could remain with those who did pray or leave quietly to go to their workplaces or for some coffee. By 8:45 the wheels of the machines were turning, and everybody was hard at work. But those few minutes at the start of the day had created an atmosphere that made Cardone Industries a very special place.

A story I picked up while talking to one of the employees told me volumes about the kind of community spirit that has been created in this place. One of the employees, a Cambodian immigrant, lost his wife in an automobile accident. The funeral for her was held right there in the chapel at the plant. That chapel has become a sacred place for this grieving widower, and the friends he has made at work are a caring fellowship with whom he can share his pain.

For me, Cardone Industries gives ample evidence that it is possible for a business to do good and do well at the same time. This company makes a lot of money, but at the same time it has created an atmosphere of concern and intimacy for its workers. The modern workplace need not be marked by the alienation and loss of personal identity that, according to sociological studies, is experienced by most people in modern industry. There can be feeling between workers. There can be a happy tone to the work day. There can be a sense of life for people who might otherwise find their jobs emotionally stifling and their capacity for passionate living just about obliterated. The workplace can be transformed into an enlivening locale where people do not have to be psychologically absent in order to be physically present. It can be a place that gives people vitality for living instead of killing them. Miracles are possible when a Christian business owner brings Jesus into the workplace.

PART X

SOME PROBLEMS ALONG THE WAY

25

Depression: The Malady of Our Time

*O*ne of the worst enemies of aliveness is depression. There are times when it overcomes us and completely obliterates our capacity to enjoy life and to drink in its glories. Depression can sometimes gain such a powerful hold over our state of consciousness that life in any form becomes unbearable. And when that happens, we may even fantasize about what it would be like simply to die. Suicide does not seem like such an evil thing at times like this.

Christianity has been sold to us as some kind of cure-all for depression so that when these bouts of despair overtake us, guilt over being depressed is added to the load we are forced to bear. Often Christian friends make matters worse with such inane admonitions as, "Where's your faith?" or "Christians aren't supposed to feel like that!" It's bad enough to be depressed without having people accuse us of being spiritually deficient on top of it all.

When it comes to this kind of misery, we have some good company. History is filled with stories of godly people who suffered from periods of depression. We cannot read the stories of the prophets Elijah and Jeremiah without recognizing that these men suffered from depressions that in today's world would have to be classified as clinical. In more recent times, the spiritual giant John Wesley, who founded Methodism, and the powerful Baptist preacher Charles Spurgeon gave ample evidence that they, too, suffered from deep depressions. But most significant of all, Jesus on the cross experienced what might be called the greatest depression that ever was. From Calvary we still can hear Him crying out to His Father: "My God! My God! Why hast Thou forsaken me?" There is no doubt that at that moment Jesus must have known a darkness in His soul so deadening that He felt abandoned, not only by the people He had come to save, but even by the One who had sent Him into the world.

Of course Jesus was only expressing His subjective feelings. The objective reality was very different. The Bible says that when He was on the cross "God was in Christ, reconciling the world unto himself" (2 Cor. 5:19). But whatever the reality on that horrendous Friday, Jesus' sense of aloneness and despair must have been complete.

When Deadness Prevails

Depression is not necessarily a spiritual malady that comes from lack of faith. It is difficult to be certain just what it is that causes depression. It seems to me and to a lot of other observers that a good number of people who ought to be depressed aren't. And there are a lot of people who will readily admit they have nothing to be depressed about but who are nevertheless living in a valley of despondency. Righteousness is no easy cure for depression.

In the Forty-second Psalm, King David let us know there were times in his life when he felt just like any of us feel when the deadness of life prevails. He knew what it was like to feel that God is far away. He wrote in this psalm that his soul longed for a taste of God, "like a deer panteth after water" (verse 1). David knew what it was like to hear from friends and foes those mocking words, "Where is your God?" (verse 3). And he knew what it is like to go to bed crying in despair and to wake in the morning with such sorrow that the morning is something to be cursed.

David, the psalmist, resonated with all of us who have been so encompassed by depression that we feel like we are drowning (verse 7). His description of depression is timeless:

> As the hart panteth after the water brooks, so panteth my soul after thee, O God. My soul thirsteth for God, for the living God: when shall I come and appear before God? My tears have been my meat day and night, while they continually say unto me, Where is thy God? When I remember these things, I pour out my soul in me: for I had gone with the multitude, I went with them to the house of God, with the voice of joy and praise, with a multitude that kept holyday. Why art thou cast down, O my soul? and why art thou disquieted in me? hope thou in God: for I shall yet praise him for the help of his countenance. O my God, my soul is cast down within me: therefore will I remember thee from the land of Jordan, and of the Hermonites, from the hill Mizar. Deep calleth unto deep at the noise of thy waterspouts: all thy waves and thy billows are gone over me. Yet the LORD will command his lovingkindness in the daytime, and in the night his song shall be with me, and my prayer unto the God of my life. I will say unto God my rock, Why hast thou forgotten me? why go I mourning because of the oppression of the enemy? As with a sword in my bones, mine enemies reproach me; while they say daily unto me, Where is thy God? Why art thou cast down, O my soul? and why art thou disquieted within me? hope thou in God: for I shall yet praise him, who is the health of my countenance, and my God. (Psalm 42)

There are those who would contend that depression is a result of our spiritual condition. And for some it may well be. But for most of us the causes of depression cannot be explained so easily.

Some Physical Causes of Depression

Some people are depressed primarily for biophysical reasons. For instance, many of us suffer depressions because of chemical imbalances or vitamin deficiencies in our bodies. As a case in point, I need go no further than my wife. Peggy had always been an upbeat and optimistic person, a ray of sunshine even on the darkest days. And then in her early fifties, there was a dramatic and painful change. A sadness came over her, and the sparkling person I had married seemed to be no more. Peggy tried counseling and that did some good, but not enough. The counselor wisely suggested that she see a doctor about estrogen replacement therapy, and she started to take hormones.

The results were startling. The depression was gone. The joy was back. My wife was her happy self once more. Peggy encourages me to tell her story in the hope that it will help someone else.

Another physically based cause of depression is lack of sleep. Scientists regularly report that many Americans are suffering from sleep deprivation. As our lifestyles have become more hectic we cut down more and more on our sleep time. This results in severe problems.

I have heard many busy people tell me they don't need much sleep. They sometimes tell me that they can get by on five or at the most six hours of sleep a night. But often these people-on-the-go are not really aware of what is happening to them. Because they do not feel physically tired and seem to be wide awake, they do not realize that their lack of sleep is influencing them emotionally and psychologically. Sleep deprivation is making them edgy, diminishing their ability to concentrate, and may be the primary source for a growing depression.

In the Bible, we read about the way the prophet Elijah confronted and defeated the prophets of the Canaanite god, Baal. In dramatic fashion he challenged the Baal worshipers to build an altar to their god while he did the same for his. Then they were to call upon their god to send fire to consume their altar while he did the same. This was putting religion to the empirical test. The people of Israel who were looking on would have a firsthand answer to the question as to which god was real and powerful.

You probably recall how the prophets of Baal called upon their god to no avail. They prayed and prayed while Elijah taunted them with such lines as, "Pray louder! Maybe your god is asleep and needs to be wakened." And, "Shout out to your god. Maybe he's away on a trip and needs to be called back."

Then it was Elijah's turn. He called upon the crowd of spectators to douse with water the stone altar he had built, just so there would be no doubt about what was about to happen. Then, while everyone stood there watching, Elijah called out to his God and got amazing results. Fire streaked down from heaven and consumed the altar.

When the people of Israel saw what had happened, they rose up and slaughtered the prophets of Baal and acknowledged Yahweh as the only true God in the land. Elijah's triumph was complete. Everything he believed in had been vindicated. His enemies were in total disarray. He had every reason to be hyper, to be on a fantastic high. But in contrast to expectations, Elijah fell into a funk. He was so depressed he could die. This prophet who knew the power of His God and how that power could be used against his enemies was more than overcome with fear at the threats posed by Queen Jezebel. He went into hiding and trembled at the prospect of what might happen to him.

It was then that Elijah called out to God, so depressed he begged to be allowed to die. God simply allowed Elijah to fall asleep. After the prophet had slept, God sent an angel to tell him to eat. To sleep and to eat! God's answers to our needs do not always come in supernatural ways.

In winning his great victory, Elijah had exhausted himself. He didn't realize it, of course, but that was because he had been on an adrenaline high in his dealings with the Baal worshipers on the mountain. But he wasn't on the mountaintop anymore, and the adrenaline that had powered his performance was dissipated. The manic time of victory was followed by a depression. His feelings were in extreme diametrical opposition to the ecstasy he had known in his moment of triumph. Biophysical realities were taking their toll on Elijah, and the once-cocky prophet became a shriveling, whining sissy.

God knew what was good for Elijah and what would snap him out of the doldrums. God knew that if Elijah slept and ate, he would feel better in the morning.

Emotional and Spiritual Causes of Depression

I don't think any of us pay enough attention to the ways in which our physical condition impacts our emotional and spiritual condition. When we fail to take care of ourselves and get proper rest, there's a price to be paid. And that price is often a full-blown depression.

It ought to be obvious to us that what happens to us spiritually can determine what happens to us physically. That's what the healings by Jesus were all about. He linked the forgiveness of sins with bodily cures. But we must also be aware that what happens to us physically can dramatically impact how we feel spiritually and emotionally. If we are going to get out of life what God intended for us to get, we had better pay attention to that fact.

Beyond the physical causes for depression there are social and psychological factors that can have a determining influence on how we feel about ourselves and the quality of the lives we are living. And of all such causes of depression, none is more significant than anger. Many people live with unexpressed anger, and it is that anger turned inwardly upon themselves that causes depression. Indeed, anger turned inward upon the self may be the most common cause of depression.

Consider the man who is slighted at work. The boss passes over him and gives the promotion he deserved to someone else. He doesn't feel appreciated, and he would quit if there were someplace else for him to go. But there is none so he goes to work hurting, and every day the anger builds. Every day it gets more intense. The poor guy can't let it out and direct it toward the person who's doing him in, so he turns the anger on himself. He hates himself instead. He condemns himself for not standing up for his rights. And he gets depressed. There can be no zest to his life nor any joyful passion in his existence. If he is ever going to regain his capacity for passion, he's going to have to deal with his anger.

I am not suggesting that this poor guy storm into his boss's office and tell him off. But he had better do something. My advice would be for him to have a conference with the boss, explain how he feels as calmly and with as much dignity as possible. In the words of Scripture, he ought not to let the sun go down on his anger (Eph. 4:26). He should put a quick end to it by expressing his sense of being treated unfairly to the one who should hear it. Let the chips fall where they may. Anything is better than letting something like this eat him up and destroy his appetite for really living.

Some older parents are angry with their children. They believe their children neglect them. They gave their kids the best they had. Maybe they didn't do everything right when they were raising their kids, but they gave it their best shot. And now their kids could not care less about them. These parents are lonely and sad; their kids could really make a difference if they cared, but they don't. Telling their kids about how they feel doesn't do any good, so the parents sit in their home and stew. Their anger makes them depressed, and the joy of living evaporates.

Let me suggest that these parents would do well to reach out to some other children. If their own children don't want their love, they ought to know that there are hordes of others who do.

I head up a missionary organization that attempts to reach out in love to children who live in America's urban ghettos. Each summer, three hundred volunteers join me in this ministry and work among these kids. The boys and girls they reach out to daily are some of the most emotionally hungry kids on this planet. Many of them are suffering from extreme parental neglect. These short-term missionaries exhaust themselves all summer long trying to love these kids into the kingdom of God.

When I ask what tires them the most, the summer volunteers always seem to tell me the same thing. "It's exhausting being with these children," they tell me. "They need so much love. They just hang all over you from morning 'til night."

So I ask you, Why should parents go on being angry with their own children and let that anger destroy them, when they could get involved in a ministry like mine and give themselves away to kids who would want their love? I've seen people with that kind of a depression come alive in wonderful ways by doing just this.

In the Forty-second Psalm, David is mad at God and actually tells off the Almighty in no uncertain terms. He says:

I will say unto God my rock, Why hast thou forgotten me? Why go I mourning because of the oppression of the enemy? (v. 9)

There are those who contend that anger against God is inappropriate, if not blasphemous. They will point out to us that we don't have any right to be mad at God. I contend that God knows when we are angry at Him, and He can take it when we need to express that anger.

A pastor friend of mine tells about a lady in his church whose little girl was diagnosed with cancer. The doctors told her that it would only be a matter of months before the child was dead. The woman left the child in her hospital bed, went down to the parking lot, got into her car, rolled up the windows tightly, and then proceeded to curse out God. She called Him every mean name she could think of. And when she finally fell silent in exhaustion, she heard a voice say lovingly and distinctly, "I'm glad you did that. It has been a long time since you spoke to Me."

The Lord can handle our anger. I'm sure He prefers to bear it rather than have us dump it on someone else or turn it in upon ourselves and be depressed. That, in case you didn't realize it before, was one of the reasons He went to the cross. When Jesus hung on Calvary's tree, he not only took our sins and guilt upon Himself; He also took our sorrows and our emotional pain (Isa. 53:4). We are told to cast all of our burdens upon Him for He cares for us (1 Pet. 5:7). "Let me be the scapegoat!" He cries out to us. And in the words of the old hymn, "Take your burden to the Lord and leave it there."

Overcoming Depression

The psalm we have been using to describe the nature of depression and to explore the anguish it can create in the soul also has some good and specific directions as to how depressions can be overcome. These instructions may be thousands of years old, but they rank far above anything you will find in those self-help books that are everywhere to be found these days. They make even some of the advice of our best psychotherapists seem superficial by comparison. But then what would you expect from the literature that God Himself inspired?

The first thing David does in the face of his depression is to remember. He remembers the good days when he was alive and joyful. He remembers the good days when God was close to Him and He worshiped Him in ecstatic joy.

> When I remember these things, I pour out my soul in me: for
> I had gone with the multitude, I went with them to the
> house of God, with the voice of joy and praise, with a multi-
> tude that kept holyday. (Ps. 42:4)

Remembering the good days may seem simple and somewhat Pollyanna-like, but let me assure you it is good treatment for depression. It is a good idea to go for a walk by yourself and to recall those days when laughter rocked your life and love flowed through you with power and intensity. To let the joyful past invade the gloomy present may be the smartest thing you can do during a time of depression.

Sometimes it does a lot of good to get together with old friends or relatives and rehash the past, remembering the good old days. Because

I am Italian, getting together for this kind of storytelling was a big part of my growing-up days.

The times I remember most were Sunday evenings. My favorite uncle and aunt would come with their children to visit us after evening church, and together with my parents, my sisters, and me would sit around the dining-room table and tell stories. Hours would pass and no one would notice. The stories were so wonderful and such fun. I can remember laughing so hard my sides felt like they would split. It wasn't just the stories; it was the way they were told. There were expressive gestures, and there was drama. And through it all there was a rebirth of the wonder of bygone days. We never ran out of stories because the charm of it all was in the telling of the same stories over and over again. Of course, the stories really weren't the same because, in the successive telling, they would be expanded and embroidered and made better and better.

With the telling of the stories, the present disappeared. All that was felt was the joy of those wonderful times that make up the oral history of a close-knit family. In the end, what is a family besides its stories?

As a preacher I use stories all the time, and those who hear me wonder where I get them. The answer is, in my everyday life. They are ordinary things lifted up in a story and made to seem wonderful. Learning how to do that may be one of the most precious things I got from my family. Once, when my son was still a boy, a featurewriter from a Christian magazine got him aside and asked him directly, "Are all those stories your father tells in his sermons true? You were with him in many of them, so you should know."

My son's answer showed wisdom beyond his years. He said, "Of course they're true. But Dad remembers big."

And that's how it was with King David. In the midst of his depression, he remembered big. He remembered when he was the leader of the band. He recalled how he led the way as the people of God danced into the temple to celebrate their God. David remembered the laughter, and he remembered the joyful soul that had once been his.

When I was a kid, we used to sing a gospel song that went like this:

When upon life's billows you are tempest-tossed,
When you are discouraged, thinking all is lost,
Count your many blessings, name them one by one,
And it will surprise you what the Lord has done.

It may sound simple, but it is not simplistic. The memories of the past can have an incredible power to dispel some of the depressions that haunt the present.

The second thing that we learn from Psalm 42 is that even in his depression King David affirms that he knew that this, too, will pass. He knows the day is coming when he will laugh again and love again and once again be able to seize the moment with passion.

My friend Barbara Johnson, who has become one of the most popular Christian writers of our time, knows depression more than most. She lost a son in Vietnam, and another son was killed by a drunk driver. Her husband was seriously brain-injured in an automobile accident and, on top of all that, she found out that another son was homosexual. Today Barbara's husband helps her with Spatula Ministries, her ministry to Christian parents of homosexual children. There have been no easy solutions to her own problems, and yet she has learned to live again, and to live with real excitement. She says that one of the things that keeps her going is that simple Bible phrase, "and it came to pass . . ."

When I asked her how she found so much hope in that little phrase, she said, "Simple! It says 'it came to pass'—it doesn't say it came to stay." When depression seems like it's always going to be a part of life, we must remember that this, too, will pass.

When Victor Frankl, the great Jewish psychotherapist from Vienna, was imprisoned in Auschwitz during World War II, he survived by making the future, with all of its possibilities for glory, more real than the present. While trapped in that nightmarish Nazi concentration camp, he carefully studied and kept notes on the others around him. What he found was that among those who escaped the crematorium, the difference between those who survived and those who died was not in their physical health or strength. Instead it was primarily dependent upon their ability to imagine a future that would express the joys of *Shalom*, which means the peace and joy of God. Those who could see beyond the present and whose hope for a better day remained undaunted were the ones with the best chance to make it through that hell.

Jesus Himself had His times of depression and despair. The night before His death was the beginning of His sufferings. Before the cross He would know an unmatched loneliness and an unrivaled betrayal by friends. But Jesus got through it. He came out on the other side as *Christus Victor*. And the basis of His survival was his clear vision of a future in which our salvation would be an accomplished fact. The Scriptures say:

> Who for the joy that was set before him endured the cross, despising the shame, and is set down at the right hand of the throne of God. (Heb. 12:2)

One of the things that makes us human is that we are the one species in God's creation with the capacity to envision the future. Therein lies the basis of our anxiety, as suggested earlier. But therein also lies the basis of our glory. We can know that the depression of the now will be dispelled; it will pass. Then we will once again know the ecstasy of the glorious life that Christ wills for His people.

The psalmist declares one last thing in the midst of his depression. He vows that he will continue to love his God and serve Him. That is something he can do in the present to escape from the depression that has sucked the passion out of his life.

We all have to learn that in the ugly here and now there is much we can do to drive away the blues. Few people on the contemporary scene have shown us this more clearly than one-time televangelist Jim Bakker.

When Jim Bakker committed adultery and then had his scandalous behavior and the financial improprieties of his organization revealed in news headlines, many of us figured he would never survive. Making it through the ordeal of the trial and imprisonment that lay ahead would, we thought, be too much for him to handle. His whimpering and sobbing as he was dragged from the courtroom was pathetic, to say the least.

And who can forget the picture of him curled up in the corner of his cell in a fetal position?

But Jim Bakker didn't crack. He didn't die, even though he may have wanted to. Today, though still in prison, he seems to be alive again in soul and spirit. Even though his wife deserted and divorced him, he has come through his time of darkness and once again is walking in the light.

In prison Jim Bakker could have withered up and died. Instead he found an opportunity there to express a new love for God by loving and serving the men around him. Instead of focusing on himself and how far he had fallen, he turned his attention to the needs of the other prisoners. He has run Bible studies and done drug counseling. He has tried to help fellow prisoners who have addictions to smoking and alcohol. Every day has become a day for Jim Bakker to love His God by serving God's people.

When some reporters tried to get the scoop on Jim Bakker's condition while in prison, they were more than surprised by what they found. His cellmate called him "real" and said he was a faithful follower of Christ. Many other prisoners gave testimonies as to how he had helped them.

It was obvious that in prison Jim Bakker, like many Christians before him, had found a new mission field. While his new ministry does not have the high profile that marked his work on the "PTL" television show, it is probably more important and surely more sincere. Jim Bakker may not have beaten the rap that the court laid on him, but he certainly has beaten a depression that could have destroyed his capacity for being emotionally alive.

Loving God is loving His people. Jim Bakker is doing that; he has rediscovered the way to be alive in Christ after most people had written him off.

People are not the victims of fate they sometimes make themselves out to be. As Cassius says to Brutus in Shakespeare's *Julius Caesar*, "Our fate, dear Brutus, lies not in our stars, but in ourselves." Whether or not we allow depression to rule our lives is largely up to us. We can use the past to drive it away. We can use the future to impact it with hope. And in the present, we can choose to do those things that will change our dispositions. What we do influences what we feel. And that is our good fortune, because that gives us control over our emotional destiny.

26

Stress: Why We're Tired All the Time

*I*t is hard to feel anything good when you're stressed out. Unfortunately, stress seems ready to overtake us every day in everything we do. Even when we vacation and try to relax, we maintain attitudes and dispositions that make for stress. I remember being uptight and tense during a short holiday at the seashore and having my wife say to me, "Relax!"

When I said, "I can't," she said, "Force yourself."

That little episode says it all. Even when we try to take it easy, we are nervous about it and even a bit guilty about not being back at the office attending to the essential details of business. We don't seem able to lay aside the tensions of our lives and just enjoy ourselves.

When Jesus talks about the kingdom of God and how we should live if we are to be citizens of it, he directs us to relax in the face of the obligations and responsibilities of life:

> And he said, "So is the kingdom of God, as if a man should cast seed into the ground; And should sleep, and rise

night and day, and the seed should spring and grow up, he knoweth not how. For the earth bringeth forth fruit of herself; first the blade, then the ear, after that the full corn in the ear." (Mark 4:26–28)

Here Jesus makes it clear that kingdom people do their job as best they can in the time that is given, and then know how to walk away from it all and enjoy some rest and restoration. God's people are able to enjoy a sabbath, even if it's not on a Sunday. They are people who can go to sleep and stay asleep without waking up every few hours having a hundred and one worries and concerns on their minds. The man in this parable has done what he was supposed to do; then he left things in God's hands to let God do what only God can do. That is the secret of his non–stressed-out existence.

In the Sermon on the Mount, Jesus spells out for us the overall disposition toward life that He wills for His people:

"Therefore I say unto you, Take no thought for your life, what ye shall eat, or what ye shall drink; nor yet for your body, what ye shall put on. Is not the life more than meat, and the body than raiment? Behold the fowls of the air: for they sow not, neither do they reap, nor gather into barns; yet your heavenly Father feedeth them. Are ye not much better than they? Which of you by taking thought can add one cubit unto his stature? And why take ye thought for raiment? Consider the lilies of the field, how they grow; they toil not, neither do they spin: And yet I say unto you, That even Solomon in all his glory was not arrayed like one of these." (Matt. 6:25–29)

This life prescribed by Jesus is lived out with an awareness of how useless stress is and how little is accomplished through worry.

As we read through the Gospels, we find that Jesus is constantly warning us against letting what he calls "the cares of this world" choke out our spirituality and our zest for life (Matt. 13:22). It is clear from the Scripture that materialism is a primary cause of stress. The worries that come from having a vast array of unnecessary things puts us on edge and keeps us from enjoying life.

Taking care of our "things" takes huge amounts of time. We kid ourselves into thinking that money is freedom, but in reality the more money we have, the more things we buy, and then we have to spend time taking care of them. Keeping the grass cut and our houses painted and in good repair takes time. Seeing to it that our cars are washed and that all the things we have are maintained takes more time. And in the midst of all this, it is easy to deceive ourselves and not realize that all the things we possess really enslave us. Like the rich young ruler described in Mark 10, we are not free to follow Jesus because we have "great possessions." The strange thing is that we seldom see this. Jesus talks about "the deceitfulness of riches," and the accuracy of this description would become obvious if we would just take a good look at our lives. If nothing else, those who accumulate wealth must spend huge amounts of time simply filling out those long income tax forms mailed to us annually by the IRS.

Beyond the sheer exhaustion that many of us experience in attending to the cares of this world, there is the added tension that always comes to those who have wealth and power because people will never leave them alone. The phone is always ringing, and someone always wants an appointment. You don't have to be paranoid to think that people are always after you. If you have money, they really are! You will find yourself being solicited for everything and anything. You will find yourself sitting and listening to pitches from people who will bore you out of your skull. The phone will ring off the hook with people who claim to know you. And just about every call and every visit will be from people who want something from you.

Tevya, in the musical *Fiddler on the Roof*, thought that being bothered like this would be fun. Maybe it is for a little while; but what Tevya didn't know is that it never stops. It relentlessly drives you into a state of edginess. Even worse, this edginess carries over into your supposedly "off" hours. You can't relax even when you try to go on vacation. The stressed-out person gets everybody up early the day of the departure, lines up the kids, and barks out orders like a drill sergeant: "Now hear this! The car is packed and ready to go! When you get into that car two things will be true: the gasoline tank will be full, and your bladders will be empty! And then we will drive and drive and drive until two things will be true: the gasoline tank will be empty and your bladders will be full! And if your bladders should be full *before* the gasoline tank should be empty, may God have mercy on your soul."

That having things makes for stress was brilliantly illustrated for a friend of mine who had to take a bus trip across central India. He was in one of those old-model buses that should have been retired a decade ago; it was seemingly held together with string and glue. As is often the case with buses in Third World countries, this bus was packed, not only with people, but with packages, furniture, and just about every kind of domesticated animal.

Sitting across the aisle from my friend was a very tired man whose neatly wrapped package sat on the luggage rack over his head. The old man wanted to yield to the sleepiness that was threatening to overtake him, but he couldn't for fear that while he was asleep, someone might take his package.

As he rode along, the old man would doze off from time to time. Each time that happened, he would wake with a sense of terror that his package might be stolen. He would quickly jerk his head sideways so he might check things out and make sure the package was still there.

That went on for hours. Then as the man snapped out of one of his tense and momentary catnaps, he looked up to find that his precious package was gone. Momentary panic crossed the old man's face as he realized he had been robbed. Then he smiled to himself, leaned back in his seat, totally relaxed, and fell into a prolonged and delicious sleep.

Being relieved of the thing that had caused him constant nervousness, he had enough sense to enjoy being unencumbered. Not many of us are that smart.

Breaking the Hold This World Has on You

To reduce the level of stress in your life, take a look at your lifestyle. Have you allowed yourself to be sucked into a pattern of constantly upping your lifestyle as your economic fortunes have increased? Are you one of those persons who is always moving up to a better house, buying better cars, and getting more and better clothes with every raise you get?

I live near the college where I teach, which happens to be in the wealthy Philadelphia suburb referred to as the "Main Line." Those who live around me are among the most successful people in America. But surprisingly, many of my neighbors are living lives that are fiscally precarious. Over the years I have seen many of them crash when there is a sudden loss of income and "the good life" they had is abruptly ended. They seem to spend right up to the level of their income, and then some. The more they earn, the more they spend. In spite of all the money they have, they tend to live beyond their means. Their lifestyles often strain their incomes. So many of them seem to have fallen victim to the tyranny of constantly striving for the next socioeconomic level, which is a always just a little beyond what they can afford.

These neighbors usually show the signs of stress. They know that at any moment their companies could announce a reorganization that would make them redundant, and if that happens they will face disaster. There are enough cases of just that happening around them to keep the fear constantly alive. There is always some unfortunate person whose sudden reversal has caused his or her house to be put on the market while the neighbors whisper to each other about how sad it all is.

A Christian response to this condition is to establish a clear definition of just what it would take to live comfortably. Then commit yourself to living at that standard, no matter how much money you make. To those who say it's all relative, I have to say that it's not. A working car that isn't a rusted-out bomb is one thing. A luxury car like a Jaguar is another. It's reasonable to have enough to eat and decent-looking clothes to wear, but insisting on eating gourmet food all the time and keeping up with all the styles is decadent. In short, life should be defined in the simplest terms possible. A simple lifestyle not only makes more resources available to serve those who are in need, but it will keep you from being entrapped by a system that will prove far too stressful for your own good.

The story of the children of Israel being led through the wilderness by Moses is the story of a people who would always have *Barachah*, the biblical word for "enough." But when the children of Israel got greedy and tried to take more of the manna from heaven than they really needed, the manna rotted and began to stink. So it is with us modern day wanderers in the wilderness. We have to clearly ascertain what is "enough" and use the rest of what we get to bless others.

Don't Take Yourself So Seriously

The second lesson to be learned is not to take ourselves and our responsibilities too seriously. It has been said that if you take life too seriously, you'll never get out of it alive.

A friend of mine once gave me a great formula for overcoming stress. He said it could all be reduced to two basic principles:

Principle No. 1: Don't sweat over the small stuff.

Principle No. 2: It's all small stuff.

Whenever you're stressed out, thinking how tragedy will surely follow if everything you think is so important doesn't get done, just ask yourself, "What difference will it all make a thousand years from now?"

One evening I was overcome by a sense of anxiety and urgency about getting to a 10:00 A.M. speaking engagement in Philadelphia the following day. The problem was that I was in Los Angeles and would not be able to finish up my obligations there before 10:00 P.M. that night.

My travel options weren't too good. When I checked the plane schedules, I found that my only real option was a crazy set of razor-close connecting flights that would have me changing planes in Dallas and then again in Atlanta. But being at that engagement the next morning was seemingly so important I had to give it a try.

Every moment I was in the air, I was nervously fidgeting. I knew if any one of the planes was even a little bit late, I would miss my connections and fail to get to the speaking engagement in time. All went well—for a while. I got to Philadelphia, got in my car, and was two miles from the hotel where I was supposed to speak when I got caught in a traffic tie-up on the expressway. There I was stuck—at a standstill. I could see the hotel where I was supposed to be from where I was sitting in my car. I grew more and more tense as the ten o'clock hour came and went. Then all of a sudden I started to laugh at myself. The question, "What difference will it make a thousand years from now?" crossed my mind. And with that perspective, my ludicrous situation enabled me to actually enjoy what just a couple of minutes earlier had been killing me.

I wish I always had enough sense to look at life like that. I'd be a lot less stressed out. I wish I could learn that what I deem to be so urgent is really not going to make a great deal of difference in the long run—because in the long run, as they say, we're all dead.

I do a lot of little things these days to lessen the stress in my life. One of them is to take the phone off the hook when I am home except for those times when I feel like taking calls. Another is not to stay in my office when I have some thinking to do. And the way I travel has changed. Now I make plans to get places at least a half-hour before I really have to be there, and I spend the time after I arrive and before my appointment making phone calls. Another thing I do is to go over the list of calls that have come in, and before answering any of them, to pray for the grace not to let other people's sense of urgency become mine.

For a long time I did not sleep as well as I should because I would find myself waking up in the middle of the night remembering something "urgent" that I had forgotten to do. What I didn't realize is that I couldn't get back to sleep for fear of forgetting what it was. Everything changed for me when I put a pad and pencil by my bed so I could write down these urgent concerns and not be afraid I would forget them in the morning. When I started doing that, I found I could go back to sleep almost immediately. Furthermore, in the morning I often discovered that what I had thought was so urgent in the middle of the night proved not to be that important at all.

Finally, at the start of each day I make a list of all the things I have to do that day, and then I rank them in order of priority. I try to make sure to do first things first and let those things at the bottom of the list wait for another day if they must. I find that most of those things at the bottom of the list end up being things I eventually don't have to do at all.

When I was a kid growing up, I knew a man who loomed bigger than life to me. His name was Edwin F. Bailey, and he was the man who ran the astronomical observatory at the Franklin Institute in Philadelphia. I would go to the Franklin Institute most Saturdays just so I could spend time with him. His encyclopedic mind fascinated me. He seemed to know something about everything, and what was even more impressive, he was entirely self-taught.

I was friends with Ed Bailey right up until he died several years ago. When he was in the hospital after a serious stroke, I went to visit him. In an effort to make small talk, I told about all the places I had just been to speak and how I had come to his bedside right from the airport.

He heard me out and then said with a slightly sarcastic manner, "You go all over the world speaking to people who, ten years from now, won't remember your name, and you haven't any time left for the people who really care about you."

That simple sentence hit me hard and changed my life. I have tried to learn to set priorities and give my time to those people who are important to me and who really need me. I have decided not to let my time be used up by people to whom I make no difference while I neglect those for whom I am irreplaceable. From time to time I have to remind myself of Ed Bailey's words because too often I let people to whom I mean nothing intrude on the most sacred relationships of my life.

A friend of mine recently got a call from the White House asking him to consult with the president of the United States. He said no because it was to be on a day he had promised to spend with his granddaughter at the seashore. The nation survived without him, the president didn't miss him, and his granddaughter had some precious time with her "Pop-Pop." First things really ought to be put first.

SOME PARTING WORDS

27

An End I Hope Won't Be a Conclusion

*T*his book was meant for everyone. I wrote it to remind you that ecstasy in life, awareness of the splendors in the commonplace, and the excitement of a sense of aliveness that makes a person want to explode in grateful gratitude are gifts that all of us are meant to enjoy.

Sometimes we meet people who want to divide the world's populace into elitists, who are capable of living on a "higher ground" as the old hymn writer called it, and the rest of us, who are supposedly content with lifeless routines and the petty distractions we call "amusements." Those pseudointellectuals or counter-cultural sophomoric cynics look condescendingly at us ordinary, middle-class folk who try to live out our faith in the common arenas of life.

We are the regular people who don't make any special claims about ourselves. We trust in Jesus, try to do what's right, and pay our taxes. We serve as deacons and deaconesses, work hard, and tithe out of our monthly paychecks.

We're the brunt of a lot of jokes. Then again, we are the flying buttresses that keep society standing just by doing what we're supposed to do, day in and day out.

A student of mine, an English literature major, let me in on his disdain for the suburban row-house lifestyle his parents had embraced.

"They do the same thing day in and day out," he said. "They know nothing of the dizzy heights to which the likes of a Friedrich Nietzsche or a Lord Byron can carry us. They are characters out of a Beckett play who seem incapable of daring action. Their idea of entertainment is watching Lawrence Welk," he scoffed.

Without being too gentle, I let that student know if it weren't for those prosaic parents of his he never would have had the opportunity to know about Nietzsche and Byron. I reminded him it was that mundane job his father routinely goes to each day that pays the bills for him to read *Thus Spoke Zarathustra* and listen to Wagner's music.

What does a kid like that think? Is he totally unaware that we, too, hunger for "something more"? Doesn't he know that we, too, yearn for ecstasy? And has he no idea that we crave the passionate life as much, and maybe more, than he does? We ordinary people have dreams and visions, too, and the measure of who we are is that we are more than ready to let go of those cherished dreams and visions in order to do what has to be done, so that our kids can have theirs.

But do not pity us. We regular folk have not given up hope. We believe it's possible to come up for air and to breathe the breath of God. And we know that in the hundred and one things we do everyday there is space for the magic of unexpected joy and just enough time to sip an other-worldly nectar.

Some of us will surprise you and at middle age or even after retirement do something wild—like the middle-aged widow who volunteered to work with our missionary team in Haiti even though she had to learn how to ride a motorcycle on mountain trails to take the job. Young people, don't be surprised if you find out someday that some of us were just waiting for you to get out of the house before we embraced the "Mission Impossible."

But even those of us who do not go awandering may have some surprises for you up our sleeves. Many of us are quite capable of blooming right where we are planted. And we just may have the gift of doing ordinary things in an extraordinary way. A hundred years ago the Danish writer Soren Kierkegaard described such a person in his classic *Edifying Discourses*. He called this person "the Knight of Faith":

> The moment I set eyes on him I instantly push him from me, I myself leap backwards, I clasp my hands and say half aloud, "Good Lord, is this the man? Is it really he? Why, he looks like a tax-collector!" However, it is the man after all. I draw closer to him, watching his least movements to see whether there might not be visible a little heterogeneous fractional telegraphic message from the infinite, a glance, a look, a gesture, a note of sadness, a smile, which betrayed the infinite in its heterogeneity with the finite. No! I examine his figure from tip to toe to see if there might not be a cranny through which the infinite was peeping. No! He is solid through and through. His tread? It is vigorous, belonging entirely to finiteness; no smartly dressed townsman who walks out to Fresberg on a Sunday afternoon treads the ground more firmly, he belongs entirely to the world, no Philistine more so. One can discover nothing of that aloof and superior nature whereby one recognizes the knight of the infinite. He takes delight in everything, and whenever one sees him taking part in a particular pleasure, he does it with the persistence which is the mark of the earthly man whose soul is absorbed in such things. He tends to his work. So when one looks at him one might suppose that he was a clerk who had lost his soul in an intricate system of book-keeping, so precise is he. He takes a holiday on Sunday. He goes to church. No heavenly glance or any other token of the incommensurable betrays him; if one did not know him, it would be impossible to distinguish him from the rest of the congregation, for his healthy and

vigorous hymn-singing proves at the most that he has a good chest. In the afternoon he walks to the forest. He takes delight in everything he sees, in the human swarm, in the new omnibuses, in the water of the Sound; when one meets him on the Beach Road one might suppose he was a shopkeeper taking his fling, that's just the way he disports himself. . . . Toward evening he walks home, his gait is indefatigable as that of the postman. On his way he reflects that his wife has surely a special little warm dish prepared for him, e.g. a calf's head roasted, garnished with vegetables. . . . He lounges at an open window and looks out on the square on which he lives; he is interested in everything that goes on, in a rat which slips under the curb, in the children's play, and this with the nonchalance of a girl of sixteen. And yet he is no genius, for in vain I have sought in him the incommensurability of genius. In the evening he smokes his pipe; to look at him one would swear that it was the grocer over the way vegetating in the twilight. He lives as carefree as a ne'er-do-well, and yet he buys up the acceptable time at the dearest price, for he does not do the least thing except by virtue of the absurd. And yet, and yet I could become furious over it—for envy, if for no other reason—because the man has made and every instant is making the movements of infinity. With infinite resignation he has drained the cup of life's profound sadness, he knows the bliss of the infinite, he senses the pain of renouncing everything, the dearest things he possesses in the world, and yet finiteness tastes to him just as good as to one who never knew anything higher, for his continuance in the finite did not bear a trace of the cowed and fearful spirit produced by the process of training; and yet he has this sense of security in enjoying it, as though the finite life were the surest thing of all. And yet, and yet the whole earthly form he exhibits is a new creation.

In the final analysis, this book has been nothing more than a guide for those who seek to become such knights. It is meant for everyday people who, behind their ordinary role-playing, have not forgotten what it is like to taste some wonder.

I know a plain, ordinary couple who live in Chicago. They go to a Presbyterian church. They have barbecues in the backyard, and their idea of a vacation is camping out. He works in a downtown office. She does what a lot of good women do—she takes care of their kids and makes a home for her husband.

If you were to ask this couple what they do that in any way contributes to the kingdom of God, they would probably tell you, "Not much."

But what they would fail to mention is that they send seventy-five dollars a month to Compassion International and support three kids in Mexico.

Compassion International is one of those organizations that links needy children in Third World countries with people in the United States who are willing to support them to the tune of twenty-five dollars a month. That's less money than it costs to buy a cup of coffee each day. But it's just enough to feed, clothe, educate, and evangelize one of those kids who lives in the barrio near Tijuana. Seventy-five dollars takes care of three of them.

Now that might not seem like much to people who revel in the belief that they are a rare breed who know all about passionate living. This couple's life may seem dull to the Jonathan Livingston Seagulls of the world.

But I am convinced of this—that one day, some day, these two calm and even-keeled Christians will stand before a judgment seat, and they will hear their Master say, "Well done, thou good and faithful servants." And if, on that day, they say, "But Lord, we never really lived life to its fullest, nor did we seize the day when we could have," He probably will smile benevolently and say, "Come on in and stay awhile. That's what eternity's for."

This book is meant for us regular people who still believe that the miraculous is a hidden dimension of the mundane and would like to figure out how to touch and taste it. It is nothing more than a collection of tips on spirituality for people who want to stay alive until they die and who want to seize the only lives they have to live and fill them with passion.

This book is the reflections of a guy pushing sixty who says about his life what that great American philosopher, Yogi Berra, once declared: "It ain't over 'til it's over."